# What It Means
# to Be a
# Man of God

MARION J THOMAS II

ISBN 978-1-68570-181-9 (paperback)
ISBN 978-1-68570-182-6 (digital)

Christian Faith Publishing
832 Park Avenue
Meadville, PA 16335
www.christianfaithpublishing.com

Printed in the United States of America

# CONTENTS

To
Cassie
You are a beautiful
soul who have made me
Feel Welcome since our
First Encounter at Fountain
Glen Temecula. I pray this
Book Bless you in every area
of your Life over into Abundance
with Joy, Peace and Great
Health and Great Wealth.

— Marvel —

Author of What it means to
be a Man of God

April 24th, 2023

Inspired by *God*

# PART 1

# Getting to Know God

When you think about the fact of getting to know the creator of the universe, who is *God*, one must know the character of *God*. Now just to be clear, no one can really know, in the sense of comprehending all that *God* is. However, we can know the essence of *God* by knowing the character of *God*. We can know the character of *God* by knowing his MO, his method of operation, when we choose to spend time purposefully and deliberately in studying the Word of *God*, accompanied also by having a purposeful, determined prayer life, which will ignite an undeniable, meaningful relationship with *God*. Yet there is another facet of the component of getting to know the character of *God*—it is by bringing your flesh under submission by deliberately fasting by making sacrifices in denying our flesh its cravings, whether it's food, social media, TV, or any other distractions that will prevent our inner spirit man from being in total control of our life!

We do this by denying the flesh all of its cravings, for there is a battle of the spiritual and the natural. Why is there a battle? Because the flesh wants to be in total control at all times. This is why Apostle

Paul stated in the Scripture, "Since we live by the Spirit. Let us keep in step with the spirit" (Galatians 5:25 NIV).

Listen, for Apostle Paul to boldly make this statement and, men, for you and me to make this same bold statement. Well, we must do what Paul did. What did Paul do? You asked? Let's go to the scriptures and find out what the Word of *God* said Paul did. "I affirm by the boasting in which I have in Christ Jesus our *Lord*, I die daily" (1 Corinthians 15:31 NKJV).

Listen, we as men must be willing to do this in order to grow closer to Christ. Our flesh must be subject to our spirit man. As I mentioned earlier, this is a war going on inwardly with our inner man and our Spirit Man. There must be a choice that we as men must be willing to make in order to activate a download of impartation from *God*, which will flow through our spiritual conduit when we remove the blockage from all the world distractions! Then we will hear from *God*, which will cause us to be spiritually connected to the only wise *living God*! (Reference from the book of Jude.) In fact, the Scripture bears witness of this fact in the book of John in the fifteenth chapter, which illustrates a vineyard, and the branches in the vineyard represent you and me (mankind), and we are attached to the vine, which represents *God*. So based on that fact, we cannot be productive outside our connection to the vine. We must stay attached to the vine if we are to make an impact in our families, in our communities, in our church, and, ultimately, outside the four walls of the church by going into the world. This is the only way we men can function and carry out the commands of *God* as the man of *God*.

In fact, the Scripture makes this abundantly clear to us as men. Here's what the Scripture states what the *Lord* is saying, "Remain in Me, and I will remain in You, no branch can bear fruit by itself, it must remain in the vine. Neither can you bear fruit unless you remain in me" (John 15:4 NIV). The text gives clear indication on what Jesus was clearly communicating to us, which is, as Christians, we are to remain attached to our source which is the *living God*! Men, we must stay connected to *God* as I indicated earlier! He is our lifeline, for the vine represents *God*. Listen, in this same text—one of most powerful statements that Jesus said in the scriptures concerning our spiritual attachment to the vine was this:

> Greater love has no one has than this, that he lay down his life for his friends. You are my friends, If you do what I command, I know longer call you servant, because a servant does not know his master business. Instead, I have called you friends, for everything that I learned from my father I have made known to you." (John 15:13–15 NIV)

Wow! Now wait a minute! Let's chew on this for a minute, men. Imagine that—if we as men remain in Jesus, that will cause him to remain in us! Jesus makes this bold proclamation saying, "Because you have remained steadfast in me, I'm going to give you a supernatural promotion that nothing on earth can rival with this." Men, are you getting as excited as I am? Let me repeat what Jesus is saying to us—Jesus Christ is saying to all men who will remain in him that we are no longer called servants, we are now called friends of *God*! Now try to grasp what this means. Jesus goes on to say everything that he learned from his Father! Oh! Oh! I'm getting happy, men! Now hear what Jesus is saying—that he will intentionally make it known to us as his friends. Wow! Now, if there was such a thing as being in the know, having inside knowledge or the inside track, having the scoop on some stuff, having advance information, which can change the outcome of situation, nothing in this world can compare to knowing what *God* knows! Imagine that, men—being in the know with *God*, who is omniscient, the *God* of all knowledge. Now we won't know all that *God* knows, but we will know what *God* wants us to know, which is more than enough! And what we don't know, we can trust that he knows everything! So being connected to his Son who then tells us, his friends, everything that *God* tells the Son. My *God*, we will have total access to the will of *God* for our lives. However, the key to this, men, is we must remain in him faithfully and then and only then will we be afforded this great revelation on being called a friend of *God*.

Now I want to point out the significance of being a friend of *God*. Let's define a friend. A *friend* is a person with whom you are on good terms with, who is not hostile, a person who you can rely on at all times. Now let me stop right here to expound on this definition of a friend. There is no human being that we can rely on at all times. Let's get this established before we go any further. So with this being the case, when you really think about it, only *God* can truly be defined as a friend—a friend that we as men can count on at all times. Yet because we live in natural bodies, though we're spiritual beings, we were created to be relational. So yes, we do have some very good friends, as men and women, in our lives. No question about that. These friends we have, they truly have the best of intentions. However, even our best of friends at times will fail us, though not intentionally, but even if they try hard not to fail us, they will fail us even with the best intentions. In fact, the Scripture cautions us not to put our complete trust in anyone but *God*! In the book of Proverbs, the Scripture says, "Like a bad tooth or a lame foot is reliance on the unfaithful in times of trouble" (Proverbs 25:19 NIV).

Now just to be clear on something regarding relationships born out of friendships, as I mentioned earlier, *God* created us to have godly relationships in our friendships with each other as men. In fact, there are books about iron sharpening iron, which involved men mentoring other men. I believe *God* ordained godly, mentoring relationships amongst men. What *God* is saying to us as men is that our ultimate friendship is found in Christ and only Christ. For in him, he never failed us, though we may think he is not on time when we need him, but trust that he is on time on what he wants to reveal to us—his actions. Ultimately, I believe *God* wants to get us back into the relationship which he started back in the creation of mankind.

In the book of Genesis, *God* had established a relationship with the first Adam by walking with him daily in the cool of the day. When I reflect on what that actually means to walk with *God* as men in the cool of the day as Adam did before sin entered into his life, well, just like any proper relationship, there must be time set aside to communicate with the one that we have established a *God*-given relationship with, such as your wife if you're married. She will enjoy this very much every time you guys communicate with her. In fact, she loves it! In the relationship with your children, it is also important to have an open communication as well. In other words, any important relationship, especially family, must be cultivated by setting aside time to discuss what's been going on and to find out if there is anything that needs to be addressed or simply just checking and keeping updated on current events.

Now by contrast, walking with *God* as Adam did in the cool of the day is *God* setting up the time by choosing to walk with his creation at the end of the day. *God* wants to see our productivity for the day based on our responsibilities as well as our initiative of what has transpired during the day. In other words, what challenges have we faced today as men? *God* wants to know what our greatest moments of the day are. How did we handle obstacles? How did we handle failures? Now here's the thing—*God* already knows what we have done because he is *God* of all knowing. The fact is, he loves us so much that he wants the relationship with us. *God* wants us to tell him everything that's going on in our world. He wants to know our disappointments, our successes for the day. This illustration with Adam is so important for us to understand as men to see how *God* values having a relationship with his creation—mankind. When Adam walked with *God*, he was in order and all was well. *God* placed Adam in the garden to care for it—basically to watch over it.

What *God* has created, he assigned to Adam to care for it and to tend to its upkeep. *God* never intended for us as men to be idle. *God* always called men who were being productive in the natural to be used by him in the supernatural.

Listen when we fail and sin against *God* as Adam did because he failed to obey *God's* command and take responsibility for his decisions and being accountable for his actions. We all know what happened in the garden, though Adam was influenced by Eve his wife. The command was given to Adam, and the ultimate decision was on him. So when Adam failed, he hid from *God*, along with Eve. When Adam hid, *God* spoke up and said, "Adam, where are you?" (Genesis

3:9 NKJV). Men, *God* is asking the same question today being posed to all men—where are you? *God* doesn't want us to run from him in our failures but to run to him in the midst of our failures, whether they are colossal epic failures or small failures! *God* wants us to run to him with all our failures, all our disappointments! Why? Because he knows anyway.

Remember, *God* is omniscient—meaning, he has perfect knowledge of all things. But because he desires an intimate relationship with us, no matter our faults, our failures, men, he wants us to bring it all to him so that we can learn from him and ask for his forgiveness, as well as to ask for his guidance. As the Scripture points out this fact: "Take my yoke upon you, and learn of me; for I am meek and lowly in heart: and ye shall find rest unto your souls. For my yoke is easy, and my burden is light" (Matthew 11:29–30 KJV).

We as men must accentuate the attributes of *God* by having an established intimate relationship with *God*. This is so important because the enemy, the devil, wants to destroy families. He wants to destroy the core or the head of the family the men. We have been given the mandate of being the protector, the provider, the priest of our homes, and the covering of our families, with *God* being the ultimate covering over our family. Yet for this to be active, the man must have an established relationship with the *Lord*, though we know as men that within the family, the wife, the mother, plays an integral part in the family dynamics, and they will fulfill that role as our helpmate. But, men, we have to give them something to help with, which makes us men. When we are operating as men who fearfully and faithfully have established a relationship with *God*, which is the divine order for the family, then our helpmate can see our allegiance to *God*! Now that's something for the helpmate to work with. In fact, in the marriage setting, the man has the greatest command from *God* concerning his relationship with his wife and how we as men should love our wives. "Husbands, love your wives, even as Christ also loved the church and gave himself for it" (Ephesians 5:25 KJV).

When we look at the meaning of the text and really get off in the content of the Scripture, there is a question that needs to be raised. The question is, what are you saying, Christ? Let's look at this closely, men. We are to love our wives as Christ loves the church. For us to really comprehend what that looks like, we must take another look at what makes up the church. It is the people who are the church, who are from various walks and backgrounds in life. You have different cultures, different attitudes, different issues, of course different levels of beliefs. In fact, the church has often been called a hospital full of sick people who are seeking after the great physician Jesus Christ! Men, are you getting the picture of what it means to love our wives as Christ loves the church? Remember, the church is full of sick people! With that being the case, can we be honest with ourselves? We know that everybody in church isn't loveable. Yet we, who are Men of *God*, are called to love our wives as Christ loves the church. With some of the most unlovable folks that we thought did not exist, Christ loves them like he loves us so much that we became lovable because of the love of Christ! Now mind you, these folks who were at times fickle, moody, hokeypokey, religious folks with their left foot in the church and their right foot outside the church, moving all around and shaking it all about—yet Christ loves us in all our human frailties. This scripture bears witness of this incredible perfect love of *God* toward us. "See what great love the Father has lavished on us, that we should be called children of *God*! And that is what we are!" (1 John 3:1b NIV).

This is an enormous task for us, as men, to accomplish. If we don't have Christ as the center of our lives, then we must have an established relationship with *God*! Wow! For us to love our wives as Men of *God*—like he loves the church. We must be supernaturally ordained by *God* to do just that! We can only do this by remaining connected to our source, who is Jesus Christ. We do this, men, by deliberately and purposefully spending time in the Word of *God*.

Oh! Real quick sidebar, men. (It is critical to find a wife who is equally sold out and loves *God* the way we do!) Remember, *God* never commanded the woman to love her husband. *God* said the wife shall honor and revere her husband, as spoken in the Scripture. "Your desire shall be for your husband" (Genesis 3:16 NKJV).

The Scripture also states this fact right here: "And the wife see that she reverence her husband" (Ephesians 5:33d KJV).

7

So, men, as I stated previously, we have to give them something that they want to revere, that they choose to love! The only way that will ever be possible, we must be sold out to *God* in every area of our lives. In doing so, the Holy Spirit will guide us in all truth. "He will guide you into all truth" (John 16: 13b NKJV). The Holy Spirit will guide you into finding that godly wife who is committed to loving and serving *God*! Men, that's why it is so important to get to know *God*, for our very lives depend on it, and so does our family!

For us, as men, to be able to effectively lead our families, our community, and our church, as leaders and the kings who we were ordained to be, men, we must have an established intimate relationship with *God*! There is no other way around it. We have to be about our Father's business! The only way to be about our Father's business is getting to know *God*. We do this by knowing the character of *God* and the will of *God*. Now, one may ask, how does one know the will of *God*? Once again, by spending time in the Word of *God*, you will begin to find yourselves in the will of *God*—simply by doing only what Jesus did and say, just like Jesus only did what the Father did. The fact is, Jesus made this point very clear. He gave us an excellent example in the Word of *God* for us, as men, to emulate and follow.

This is what Jesus said, "I and the Father are One [in essence and nature" (John 10:30 AMP). When we as men become one with the Father, then we can effectively carry out our *God*-given purpose. For when we embrace our roles as Men of *God* in every fabric of our society by our imprints—first in our family, in our communities, in our cities, in our church buildings—then we can impact the world as Men of *God*!

We are called to faithfully impact everywhere our foot tread as salt and light in this dark world. The Scripture is clear that when we operate in our salt and light position, we will impact this world! Let's take a look at the text.

> You are the salt of the earth. But if the salt loses its saltiness, how can it be made salty again? It is no longer good for anything, except to be thrown out and trampled underfoot. You

are the light of the world". A town built on the hill cannot be hidden. Neither do people light a lamp and put it under the bed. Instead, they put it on its stand, and it gives light to everyone in the house. In the same way, let your light shine before others, that they may see your good deeds and glorify your father in heaven. (Matthew 5:13–16 NIV)

Now, men, I want you get a visual of what Jesus was saying here. When we fail to operate as salt in this world, we become useless men in our society—good for nothing—and we will allow the devil and his imps to run roughshod, along with the world, over you! Listen, men, if we have no Holy Ghost salt in the game, it is impossible to be a light in the world that is infatuated with darkness. Salt and light are a dangerous combination to be used by *God* for his glory! Author and pastor Warren W. Wiersbe made this profound statement in his book *On Being a Servant of God*. I quote, "A Holy Minister is an awful weapon in hands of *God*" (Robert Murray M'Cheyene).

As Men of *God*, if we are to fulfill the mandate that *God* has placed upon our lives. It is essential for us to spend deliberate and purposeful time to get to know *God*, even when we don't feel the presence of *God*. For we know that the Bible tells us that *God* will never forsake us! For he himself has said, "I will never leave you nor forsake you" (Hebrew 13:5 KJV).

There is true freedom in knowing and embracing the absolute promises from *God*, knowing he will always be there for us. There is a self-assurance that we as men can be confident in the fact that *God* loves us that much! Also, how much *God* wants us to know him and all his ways, even when we don't feel his presence or comprehend his presence. We must take the posture that Job took in the Bible when he couldn't sense the presence of *God*. Job said this:

> Behold I go forward, but he is not there; and backward, But I can't perceive him; On the left hand, where he doth work, But I cannot behold

him: He hideth himself on the right hand, That
I cannot see him. But he knoweth the way that I
take; when he hath tried me, I shall come forth as
Gold. (Job 23:8–10 KJV)

So, men, in other words, *God* has already ordered our steps.
Because he has already our steps! Guess what? We will always be in
the right place at the right time. He knows the path we should take,
even before the foundation of the world! However, in order for us to
walk into our divine purpose for our lives, we must totally surrender
our lives to his will, then we will be in his divine will for our lives.
Furthermore, there will be nothing in our lives that would catch us
off guard. Why? Because everything we as men are set out to do
for *God*, he has already ordained for us to do! In fact, the Scripture
bears witness to this fact. "All the days ordained for me were written in your book before one of them came to be" (Psalm 139:16b
NIV). Our life has already been planned out, so we, too, must make
wise plans because *God* himself is very big on planning his way. The
Scripture speak on planning in the book of Luke.

Suppose one of you wants to build a tower,
Will he not first sit down and estimate the cost to
see if he has enough money to complete it? For if
he lays the foundation and it's not able to finish
it, everyone who sees it will ridicule him saying,
this fellow began to build and was not able to
finish. (Luke 14:28–30 NIV)

Now if I may, allow me to unpack these three scriptures from
the Word of *God*, which clearly outlines the biblical tenants for planning outline by *God*. The Bible clearly references that planning is in
the will of *God*. In fact, it actually promotes faith in believing in *God*
that he will honor our plans, especially when we deliberately include
*God* in the planning process. In the book of Proverbs, the text says,
"In heart of Man we set plans. But the *Lord* determines our steps!"
So we're believing and trusting *God* when we include *God* in our

plans. We pray about it while engaging in the Holy Spirit concerning our plans, which will guide us in all truth. Then we meditate on the Word of *God* day and night. By doing so, we set ourselves up to be blessed by *God*, and our plans will be blessed by *God*. This is promised in the Scripture. In the book of Joshua, it clearly states this fact! "Do not let this book of the law depart from your mouth; meditate on it day and night, so that you may be careful to do everything written in it. Then you will be prosperous and successful" (Joshua 1:8 NIV). Now look at how planning that included *God* will not only lead us to be successful because of *God* but it will also allow us to become more intimate with *God*—that would allow us to know *God* by his character, by his MO—his method of operation—also for us to get back to *God's* original plan concerning men, which is to govern *God's* creation that will bring all the glory to *God*, which he deserves! We are to emulate the character of *God* by being a giver just like *God*! We are to become conduits of *God's* blessings to become a blessing to others!

In doing so, we as men of *God* will begin to exemplify the character of *God* by demonstrating the love of *God* toward others. Our lives should be a living example to all those we become in contact with, that we may show them we belong to *God*! The lifestyle we live should reveal this to those we come in contact with—that we belong to *God*!

In other words, the way we live as men of *God* should glorify *God*. It has been said that the closest thing that some people will ever see inside a church to sense the presence of *God* is by men and women representing Christlike behavior, walking in love, and professing to know *God* as *Lord* and *Savior* and *Master* of our lives. The Scripture solidifies this on how our lifestyles are to be observed by others who see *God* in us.

> [No] You yourselves are letter of recommendation [our credentials], written in your hearts, to be known [perceived, recognized] and read by everybody. You show and make obvious that you are a letter from *Christ* delivered by us, not writ-

ten with ink but with [the] Spirit of [the] *Living God*, not on tablets of stone but on tablets of human hearts. (2 Corinthians 3:2–3 AMPC)

Now allow me to unpack the essence of this text so folks will know we belong to *God*, not by shouting hallelujah every time someone speaks to us or acting pious as if we are better than others—no, not at all. But our attitude will show that *God* still rule affairs of all men! Also, how we treat others by our words, actions, and deeds. We are *God's* representatives here on earth! We are to be leaders ordained by *God*! Listen, with truth being known, even sinners who don't know *God* are very successful in the world, simply by applying their gifts and natural talents without saying, "Thank you, *Lord*!" However, though they may be successful, they have no peace and they are never satisfied because they become overtaken by greed. The difference with those of us who are completely sold out to *God* is by surrendering our total being unto *God*, by knowing *God* through his Word, and by submitting to *God* so that we become pliable in the hands of *God*, so that we can be used by *God*! For this to be activated in our lives as men of *God* to be used by *God*, we must first surrender our will to *God*, which will enable us to obey *God*. In the book of Isaiah, three components are revealed to usher you and me to pursue *God*.

By the way, the book of Isaiah is one of the major prophets who truly captured the majestic eloquence of *God* more than any other prophet in the Bible. In chapter 9 of Isaiah, verse 6, Isaiah gave us the distinct roles of *God* outlined in this chapter. It says, "For unto us a child is born unto us a son is given and the government shall be upon his shoulder; and his name shall be called Wonderful Counselor, the Mighty *God* the everlasting *Father*, the Prince of Peace" (Isaiah 9:6 The New Scofield Study Bible). Now I'm of the mindset that before we can experience *God* as the prince of peace, we must first experience him as our wonderful counselor, then we can experience him and know him as a mighty *God*.

When we encounter him as a mighty *God*, we can now approach him and know him as an everlasting Father. Then we can now know him as our prince of peace. I will now take us to knowing him in each

WHAT IT MEANS TO BE A MAN OF GOD

of these distinctive and perfect roles—starting with knowing him as our wonderful counselor!

## Knowing God As a Wonderful Counselor

When we think of a counselor, we generally think of an individual who knows things that we may not know or are privy to or who has all the information that we need in order for us to be successful. So it's safe to say that a counselor is one who guides an individual with their best interest at heart, with the main goal which is to ensure that one has the proper tools or right information for you and me to succeed in whatever endeavors one chooses to pursue.

I can remember as far back as junior high school, starting in the seventh grade through ninth grade, which was the format back then when I attended junior high school. My seventh-grade counselor prepared me for entrance into eighth grade. There were some things that I experienced in the seventh grade that needed to be evaluated in preparation for me to be successful in my entrance into the eighth grade. When I got to the eighth grade, I was better prepared for it. Therefore, I was successful in my eighth-grade tenure. Well, the same format was instituted with my eighth-grade counselor in preparation for my entrance into the ninth grade. Now my ninth-grade counselor, at this point in my junior high school tenure, became my most important counselor. The reason why was because this counselor was preparing me for a whole different level of challenges going into my next level of high school. If you can imagine, or should I say remember, how you felt entering into high school—the feelings that went through my mind was a feeling of excitement. There was also fear of the unknown, thoughts on how can you fit in. As you know, in high school, you have an influx of students from different junior high schools from different areas in the city that I lived in, different neighborhoods from where I lived. Once again, I remind you of all these feelings coming upon you when you're transitioning from junior high school to high school. In my time, high school started at the tenth grade level as opposed to now—it starts from the ninth grade. So for me to be mentally and socially prepared. The family and the community that I serve has played an important role in my development, and I believe your family and the community you serve will serve the same purpose for your development as well. All these influences and wise counseling have imparted valuable knowledge upon you to help you face and prepare for upcoming challenges. Guess what? The journey now continues in the same format of counselors as we did in junior high school.

I now have tenth-grade counselors who welcome all the new students transitioning from junior high to high school, getting us ready for the next level—the eleventh grade. So the eleventh-grade counselor did what they did. However, each level of counselors in high school became more important than our previous counselors, though they were all important and shall not be minimized for their roles, although each level requires different counseling.

Men, you see where I'm going with this right? Well, stay with me. My twelfth-grade counselor played the most important role for the role they played—they were getting us ready for life after high school. They were getting us ready for college, trade school, evaluating our skill set and our mindset prior to leaving high school and what future expectations we had for ourselves.

Now I want to share with you, men. Though we had all this wise counseling from junior high school through high school who were preparing me to make life decisions after high school, well, guess what? All of this wise counseling from my counselors and my family were all contingent upon one thing and one thing only! Are you ready for the one thing? Well, here it is! Listening and obeying!

You see, receiving all that sound advice and great counseling didn't matter—if I was not willing and obedient to listen, I couldn't benefit from the sound counsel over the years. There are scriptures that talk about those of us who are willing and obedient. Here's what the Scripture says concerning this matter: "If you are willing and obedient, You will eat the good things of the land" (Isaiah 1:19 NIV). This same spiritual law also applies in the natural. When we obey and listen to sound counsel, we will profit greatly. You may ask this question—how can we determine when we receive sound counsel and good advice?

Well, when the counseling and advice is preparing us to excel and become better version of ourselves or to become a more successful version of ourselves without compromising our godly principles, when we know right from wrong, and when the persons or individuals doing the counseling are not looking for anything in return, whether it be monetary or in deeds, but take great satisfaction and pride in your success! Because their sole purpose is to prepare us for upcoming challenges and obstacles with success that awaits each of us when we obey wise counsel. In fact, the Scripture talks about a multitude of counselors.

"Where there is no guidance the people fall, But in abundance of counselors there is Victory" (Proverbs 11:14 NASB)! Now, with that brief but solid introduction regarding counselors, now I want to expound, if I can, with my limited knowledge on the creator of mankind who is the counselor of all counselors!

In fact, the great major prophet Isaiah refers to *God* as our wonderful counselor! There is a passage in the Bible that gives us a glimpse of this wonderment of *God*.

"But the Angel of the *Lord* said to him, Why do you ask my name, seeing it is Wonderful?" (Judges 13:18 NKJV). This particular passage was concerning the promised birth of Samson being inquired by Manoah the father. He just wanted to honor the *Lord* for when the promise became a reality. So he asked, "What's your name?" Well, men of *God*, we already know his name, and yet it is still too wonderful. Think about all the promises he came through for you, getting sidetracked, which is easy to do when the wonderment of *God* is being discussed!

Let me get back to my introduction of this wonderful counselor! Wow! What a powerful statement the *Lord* said to Manoah! Yes, the name of *God* it is too wonderful! When you meditate on the goodness of *God*, it is truly easy to come to the conclusion that *God* himself is too wonderful!

So, men, our introduction in knowing *God* is simply to know the attributes of *God*, which is to know the characteristics of *God*, which will guide us to the MO, his method of operation. And this *God* is a wonderful counselor. As I mentioned earlier, Isaiah the prophet is the only one, I believe, in the Old Testament who gives us a majestic view of the eloquence of *God*, as well as the sovereignty of *God*.

In fact, Isaiah in his writings gives us an inside view on the grace and glory of *God*. It is easy to see why Isaiah views *God* as our wonderful counselor. For we, as men of *God*, who desire to walk with *God*, must also see him as our wonderful counselor, and we must adhere to words and teachings of the scriptures in the Word of *God*. Therefore, we must surrender our entire will unto *God*. In doing so, the Scripture tells us we will be blessed by the wise counsel of *God* as the Scripture so aptly states. "How blessed is thc Man who does not walk in the counsel of the wicked, Nor stand in the path of sinners, Nor sits in seat of scoffers. But his delight is in the law of the *Lord*, and in his law he meditates day and night" (Psalm 1:1–2 NASB).

Men, the Bible clearly gives each of us the end results when we make a deliberate decision to submit ourselves to the counsel of *God*! In fact, scriptures says emphatically, "How blessed is the Man who does not walk in the counsel of the wicked," as stated in the book of Psalms. The Scripture is written for all believers concerning the gospel of *Christ*. Obviously, there are others who are not walking with *God* the *Father*. Instead, they are walking with their father the devil. But those of us who are walking under the counsel of *God*, we're also experiencing continuous joy and our minds are continually governed by the goodness of *God*! Men, don't you remember when you first fell in love with your first girlfriend or your wife? Listen, we were so much in love to the point that we would spend countless of hours over the phone, even falling to sleep on the phone, literally talking ourselves to sleep, because we were so much in love and we couldn't wait to see and talk to her again! In fact, some would say that we were sprung on them with our nose being wide open because of our love for them. We could not stop thinking of her. Well, men of *God*, we must have the same mindset when it comes to loving *God*! We must be so in love with *God* that our entire being must be evidence of it to everyone we come into contact with. Also, love him because of his goodness toward us! I love *God* because he first loves me!

In the Scripture, it is revealed to us how *God's* thoughts toward us are continuous. This scripture gives us a great analogy on how much he loves us. Men, it is revealed in this scripture text right here: "How precious also are thy thoughts unto Me, O *God*! How great is the sum of them! If I should count them, they would outnumbered the sand" (Psalm 139:17–18).

Wow! Men, think about the enormity of that scripture. Better yet, ride down to your nearest beach and walk down to the sand, then pick it up and see if you can count the grains of sand! If this doesn't make you tear up! That the creator of all mankind thinks of me like this, us like this, is love that I can't even comprehend. Why wouldn't we not want to surrender our will, our lives to *God*!

I had to pause from writing for a moment. I am just overwhelmed on how much *God* loves us! Even when we have not always been lovable and our thoughts haven't always been pure and, at times, our motives were questionable. Yet, the love of *God* is continuous toward us. One of my favorite scriptures in depicting *God* loves toward us is found in the book of Isaiah. "Though the Mountains be shaken and the hills be removed, yet my unfailing love for you will not be shaken nor my covenant of peace be removed, Says the *Lord*, who has compassion on you" (Isaiah 54:10 NIV).

It is truly remarkable to know that the *God* of the universe's thoughts toward us is constant. We're always on the mind of *God*! But in order for this love to be real in our lives, we must embrace the reality of *God's* love toward us. We embrace it by being intentional in our pursuit to go after *God*, by establishing a relationship with *God*—that even in our imperfection, we are loved perfectly by a perfect *living God*! Once this reality becomes real to us as men, we must put ourselves in the right posture to receive from *God* simply by completely obeying *God*! Our obedience to him is the key to be counseled by him.

Now for us as men to be counseled by him, we must know the voice of *God*. Though his voice may not be audible to us in terms of a voice, yet *God* knows how to speak to us. It could be by connecting to us spiritually by something we read in his Word, by a song, by the preached word, or by praying and spending time with *God*. But make no mistake—*God* knows how to get our attention. In fact, the Scripture also tells us that we, indeed, know the voice of *God*. This scripture bears witness of this fact. "My sheep hear my voice, and I know them, and they follow me" (John 10:27–28 ESV).

Let's look at the three components of this text. First, we must know his voice. Second, Jesus knows our voice. Third, we will follow him because we hear him, and we know him by immersing ourselves in reading and studying the Word of *God*. For in his Word, we will hear his voice and we will know his voice. Listen, there is nothing more important than hearing and knowing the voice of *God*. For if we know his voice, then we can't be led by the voice of the devil. When we hear *God's* voice with confidence, then we will respond to his voice!

Now his voice may not be audible. But *God* still speaks, as I have mentioned, through gospel songs, through his Word, and even in our dreams. So yes, *God* still speaks, even today! Listen, *God* truly wants to speak with us men every day.

There are things that *God* wants to show us that will usher us into his presence. Now we know in the Old Testament that *God* spoke verbally to Moses. He spoke verbally to Abraham. He spoke to the prophet Samuel. In fact, generally speaking, the prophets were the mouthpiece of *God* to get his message to the people.

The Scripture tells us that *God's* Word is a living word, "For the word of *God* is alive and active. Sharper than any double edge sword, it penetrates even to the soul and spirit, joints and marrow; it judges the thoughts and attitudes of the heart" (Hebrews 4:12 NIV). So, men, *God's* Word is not dead. It is a living word that is active in the lives of every believer who has surrendered their life to *God*. Yet for this to be a reality, there must be a total submission to the ways of *God*.

As I mentioned before, the Scripture says, "If you abide in me and my words abide in you, Ye shall ask what ye will, and it shall be done unto you" (John 15:7 KJV).

Did you just grasp that? The enormity of this scripture speaks volumes in terms of how *God* wants to be divinely connected to us through his Word. When we as men continue to abide in *God* and that *God* continues to abide in us, guess what? Now *God* can trust us with trouble, *God* can trust us not to run from him but to keep turning toward him! Listen when we as men continue to abide in *God*. Let me say this—I'm not dismissing the woman and her role to be used by *God* because *God* has certainly used women and has continued to use women in the ministry today as well, but I'm speaking to the men for we are the covering for our women—we as men must align ourselves with the divine order of *God*. If we are under the wise counsel of *God*! We must continually abide in *God*.

Now when we do, we have just repositioned ourselves to receive the greatest promotion in the history of mankind, which is recorded in the Scripture. "Henceforth I call you not servants; for the servant knoweth not what his *Lord* doeth: but I have called you friends; for all things that I have of my Father, I have made known unto you" (John 15:15 KJV). Men, are you getting this? That we are no longer called servants of the most high *God*—*we* are now called friends of *God*. We now become in the know! Listen, the world has their definition of being in the know—by having inside information that others don't have. But listen, even in that, there is no comparison of being in the know in and from *God*.

Jesus said everything that he hears from the Father, he might let us know. He will think about letting us know. No, Jesus made it emphatically clear to what he said. Jesus said, "I will let you know everything that *God* tells me." Oh, glory! Men, what a promotion in the headlines from *God*.

I remember, as child growing up in church, singing this old church hymnal "What a Friend We Have in Jesus"! Not knowing at that time, when I was singing that song in church as a child, what it truly means to have a Jesus as a friend. Well, this can truly be attainable in our lives, men, when we make a continual habitation in abiding in the Word of *God*. In doing so, we have taken the right posture in submitting to the will of *God*. Then we can now begin to experience this wonderful counselor—the only true, wise living *God*.

So when *God* speaks to us and says something as simple as, "Turn right instead of turning left," or "Don't go, say this, don't say that," when we simply adhere to these simple but powerful commands, we can then be trusted to do what doesn't make sense to us that does make sense to *God*.

Here's a great example, from the Scripture, which speaks about this. Remember in the text about this great commander who had leprosy? He was spoken to by the prophet Elisha who spoke with *God*. Here's what Elisha told this great commander—here's what you need to do to retrieve your healing. "And Elisha sent messenger to him saying, Go and wash in the Jordan seven times, and your flesh shall be restored to you, and you shall be clean" (2 Kings 5:10 NKJV). When Naaman was told what to do by the man of *God*, he became very angry. Why? Because he was told, "Wash in the dirty Jordan River," and he wanted to be healed in the way he thought he should be healed. Ask yourselves how many times we thought *God* should have answered our prayers our way instead of his way. The text goes on to say that he wanted Elisha to come to him and wave his hands and call on *God*.

He also said, "Are there cleaner waters elsewhere than Israel?" So you see, *God* wants to know we will obey him, even when it doesn't make sense to us. Listen, no matter what challenges we face. We must never forget who we are dealing with. *God* is our wonderful counselor, and he knows what to do and when to do it.

"Know that the *Lord* is *God* it is he who made us, and we are his; we are his people, the sheep of his pasture" (Psalm 100:3 NIV).

When we let *God* be *God*, we can be used by *God* for his glory.

Listen, *God* will vet us to see if we truly desire to obey him for being who he is, or do we desire him for what you desire to get from him? For if we truly desire to obey him, we will do it with all our heart, no matter what.

In doing so, we can now experience these components in our relationship with *God*. For now, we know him as an Everlasting Father and a Mighty *God*, and surely as the Prince of Peace, for we have learned to truly obey God our wonderful counselor with our whole heart no matter what.

Why? Because of his great love for us and he left us the Holy Spirit, which will guide us in all truth and nothing but the truth! The Scripture, once again, will always bear witness to the truth of *God* in everything that *God* does and tells you and me, and in regard to the guidance of the Holy Spirit, the Scripture gives us insight on the function of the Holy Spirit in the life of every believer. "The Spirit of truth comes, he will guide you into all the truth. He will not speak on his own; He will speak only what he hear, and he will tell you what is yet to come" (John 16:13 NIV).

Now if I may, allow me to unpack this wonderful revelation of *God's* message to us regarding the Holy Spirit. The job of the Holy Spirit is to get us to move in the direction that he intends for you and me as men of *God* to move in without hesitating or doubting—toward *God*. Remember when I said earlier that we are his sheep and we know his voice and he knows our cry? In fact, he knows the very hairs on our head with or without hair. He knows the exact pores on our scalp where the hair particle comes from.

Getting back to unpacking this scripture. First, the Holy Spirit will guide us in the knowledge of his truth for us. If I may use this terminology used by the world—"being in the know!" Well, it's one thing being in the know in the natural and a whole other thing being in the know in the supernatural, which is being in the know in the spiritual realm in *God*. The Scripture further tells us that the Holy Spirit will divulge to us whatever he hears from the Father.

The Holy Spirit only speaks what he is told and what he hears from the Father only and not what he thinks. Though the Holy Spirit has a seat at the table, he has no voice at the table. He only speaks what he hears and what he is told. When we get our information from the Holy Spirit, we now have access to what is to come and what to expect, not because of the wealth of information but we can rely that the information is all truth, no matter the size of the content of what was shared with us. Remember, men, we walk by faith and not by sight!

So, men, if we are given the Holy Spirit to guide us in all truth, doesn't it make sense that we spend time in the Holy Spirit by fellow-shipping with him as the Scripture commands us to do? "The grace of the *Lord Jesus Christ*, and the Love of *God*, and the commune of the Holy Ghost, be with you all. Amen" (2 Corinthians 13:14 KJV).

The Scripture clearly indicates our role in this relationship with the Holy Spirit. We must purposely fellowship with the Holy Spirit where it becomes a way of life for every child of *God* and not check something off like we check off on a checklist. Because of our love for *God*, it will lead us and direct us into the abundant life of knowing Christ personally and intimately. However, the only way, men, we can experience this abundant life in Christ is we must have surrender life unto Christ.

A surrendered life is simply translated to being yoked up with the life of Christ. Now here's the thing, men, either you're yoked up with Christ or you're yoked up with the devil! Either way, a yoke is involved. Now the choice is up to you. You can choose to be yoked up with the creator of all mankind and the entire universe or yoke up with the devil who is already a defeated foe! Now reading what you just read, you may be saying to yourself, "Why would I want to be yoked up with a loser who is destined to be bound in hell for eternity?" Now as crazy as the latter sounds, there are many, many, people, men and women, who don't believe *God*, so, therefore, they are yoked up with their father the devil, so disobeying *God* by default causes you to obey the devil, the father of all lies!

How many times have you heard people say that being a Christian is hard work; well, on the contrary, being a sinner is the hard life, even though they may think they are winning. Why? Because sin is fun, yet it is all temporal. The Scripture indicates differently on the life of a Christian as opposed to the life of a sinner. "Good understanding giveth favor: but the way of the transgressors is hard" (Proverbs 13:15 KJV).

This scripture speaks to two groups of folks! The first part of the scripture speaks to those who choose to obey *God*. Those who choose to obey *God* will receive good understanding, along with favor, from *God*. Now the second part of the text speaks to these group of folks who choose to disobey *God*, which says, "The way of the transgressors is hard." The one common denominator that both groups have in common is this—it's a choice!

So yes, it is a hard life of disobeying *God*. Though you may be rich and very successful, yet you have no peace, never satisfied, and have no real joy. It's artificial happiness—you can't trust anyone! Now that's a hard life to have despite being so rich. However, to those of us who choose to obey *God*, we have access to the abundant life full of joy from *God* and not from the world, not free of trouble but constant peace and joy, along with favor from *God*. Now I want you to know that this joy and peace and favor does not depend on the size of our bank account or the size of our homes or the cars we drive or the diamonds. No, sir! No, ma'am! It is only because of how big our *God* is and the intimate relationship we have with him. However, *God* doesn't mind if we have those things as long as those things don't have us! *God* must be first priority of our lives, men, and because of our relationship with *God*, it will make us content, no matter our social status in this life. Listen, as I just stated, *God* doesn't mind us having riches as long as riches don't have us. *God* must have our ear; if he has our ear, he can speak into it. When *God* has our heart, he can pour into it. Then our walk with *God* would exemplify what it means to be yoked up with *God*, as I have shared with you earlier. Here's what the Scripture says about it when you and I become yoked up with *God*: "Take my Yoke upon you and learn from me, For I am gentle and lowly in heart, and you will find rest for your souls" (Matthew 11:29 KJV).

So, men, being yoked with *God*, if we choose to obey him, is inevitable, which will lead to a life of joy, peace, healing, and favor. Men, when you think about what it means to be yoked up to *God*, it means that when we walk with *God* and he says go right, we go right, and when he says go left, we go left. For *God* knows what we need and when we need it. If I may use the analogy of a parade. There is the beginning of the parade, there is the middle of the parade, and there is the end of parade.

Life can be a parade, men. But here's the catch—we can't see the middle of the parade or the end of the parade. Only *God* can see the whole parade. For *God* can see every angle, every turn, every obstacles, every hidden danger. We can't see past tomorrow or, for that matter, the next hour of our lives—certainly, we can't see none of those things—yet when we find ourselves being yoked up with *God*, we don't have to be concerned with life's parade and the different turns that life holds for us.

Why? Because our trust is in the hands of the one who knows all of our tomorrows and all of our days. The Scripture lays this out for us too. "All the days ordained for me were written in your book before one of them came to be" (Psalm 139:16b NIV).

Wow! Men, what a fabulous journey in getting to know *God*! Men of *God*, are you excited and ready to proceed? I am!

In the next chapter, we will explore discovering the essences of *God* through the scriptures! Ready, let's go!

# PART 2

# Discovering the Essences
# of God Through Scriptures

I n discovering the true essence of *God*, one must determine the meaning or definition of the word *essence*.

The word *essence*, according to the *Random House Webster's Unabridged Dictionary*, is defined as the Greek word *philos*, which means "it's the inward nature, the true substance of a matter." In other words, "the invariable nature of a thing." Now when we as men look at how this applies to us and when it is applied to the nature of *God*, it's different as night and day. Though we are housed in a physical body, yet we are spiritual in our very core. Or we can say that invariable thing is the essence of our nature, which is our spiritual being existing in an earthy body. But *God* himself is spiritual through and through. He is a supernatural being. You see, *God* is self-containing, *God* is self-existing. He is the beginning and the end of a thing. The essence of *God* can only be defined by knowing the characteristics of *God*.

Now to know the characteristics of *God* is to look at the various postures of *God* or the personalities of *God*. Well, for one, we know by the self-existence of *God* that he is known as an omniscient *God*. The all-knowing *God*—in other words, the *God* who knows everything, even before things were in existence or before it came to be. In fact, the Scripture bears witness of this being one of the very natures or postures of *God*. That *he* is an all-knowing *living God!* "Before a word is on my tongue you, *Lord*, know it completely" (Psalm 139:4 NIV). Here's another confirming scripture that the text reveals that he is an all-knowing *God*. "In whatever our heart condemns us; For *God* is greater than our hearts and knows all things" (1 John 3:20 NASB). Let me go further in uncovering the other natures of *God* as in three natures in one being. The trinity of *God* as in *Father*, the *Son* and the *Holy Spirit* are the three distinct attributes of *God* in the one person of *God*.

*God* is also known an omnipotent *God*, the *God* of all power, which can be easily described as *God* is a superior supreme being with supreme power that has no limitations. The Scripture also bears witness of this fact as well regarding the all-surpassing power of *God*. "Behold, I am the *Lord*, The *God* of all flesh. Is there anything too hard for Me?" (Jeremiah 32:27 NKJV). Here's one of my favorite scriptures in depicting the eternal power of *God*. "And his radiance of his glory and the exact representation of his nature, and upholds all things by the word of His power" (Hebrews 1:3a NASB).

Men of *God*, are we getting the picture of who we're dealing with here? For he is *God*, and he is *God* all by himself! Oh, glory! Let's recap what we discovered thus far. We got a glimpse of *God* as being an omniscient *God*. We saw him as an omnipotent *God*. Now let us look at a third component of his nature as an omnipresent *God*.

He is a *God* who is everywhere at all times—at the same time, with no limitations in his ability to be all knowing and to be everywhere at the same time. These two scriptures I will present to you now, as if I'm in the court of law proving the power of *God*. But first, let me say this, though there are many more evidence of scriptures that I can present, yet these two speak volumes. Here is the first one.

> Where can I go from Your Spirit? Or where can I flee from your presence? If I ascend to heaven, You are there, If I make my bed in sheol, Behold you are there. If I take the wings of dawn, If I dwell in the remotest part of the sea, Even there Your Hand will lead me, And your right hand will lay hold of me. (Psalm 139:7–10 NASB)

In the book of Job, he makes it clear. "For his eyes are upon the ways of a man, And He sees all his steps" (Job 34:21 NASB). So now that we have explored the essence of *God* being on display in the text, looking at the attributes of *God* through scriptures as I have pointed out to you—one, that he is a *God* of all knowing, two the *God* of all power, three, he is a *God* who can be everywhere at the same time, without limitations in each of his natures.

Now, men, if you can just allow the enormity of what you just read in regard to those three components of *God*. I'm reminded of what the major prophet Isaiah on what he had to remind the people who they were dealing with. We, too, must never forget who we are dealing with when we deal with *God* going forward in 2022, especially in this pandemic season. The prophet Isaiah pose this question right here to the people as if *God* himself was asking the question, "Have you not known? Have you not heard? Has it not been told you from the beginning? Have you not understood from the foundations of the earth? It is he who sits above the circle of the earth" (Isaiah 40:21–22 NKJV). In case we still haven't figure it out, what Isaiah was asking according to this text:

> Lift up your eyes on High and see who has created these stars, the Holy One who leads forth their host by number, he calls them all by name, because of the greatness of His might and

the strength of his power, Not one of them is Missing. (Isaiah 40:26)

Now, men, to bring this text into full revelation of what this text is saying and the enormity of what this scripture is saying and what it means to us as men, allow me to unpack the text. The cripture says that *God* created the stars and knows them by name and goes on to say that not one is missing, plus he knows every single one of them. Let me put this in perspective regarding the stars.

According to *UCSB Science* in the Google application, there are about ten billion galaxies. I quote from UCSB in the observable universe, which leads to this number of one hundred billion stars per galaxy—meaning, one billion trillion stars in the universe! Wow! Men, did you hear what I said, even though I just wrote it?

Over one trillion billion stars, and it is *God* who created every single star, and he knows every single star by name. Listen, not only does he know all trillion billion stars but he goes on to say, "Not one is missing!" *I said, not one is missing*! You heard me? My *God*! Now, do you know? Now, have you heard? Now ask yourself, what kind of *God* do you serve? Now I'm assuming that each of you has a relationship with *God* the creator of the universe and the creator of mankind. Well, if you do not have a relationship with *God*, now ask yourself, what does it mean for you if you have a relationship with *God*? Since we are ordained to be *God's* representatives in the world! And we should be.

If so, now that we look at what the essence of *God* looks like in terms of his perfect holy character, it truly behooves each of us to have an established relationships with *God*. With this being the case, nothing in this life could satisfy us and nothing in this life would be difficult for us to withstand. Even though we have an established relationship with *God*, we still go through the storms of life. Yet though we're in the storm, we have the peace of *God*, even while we're in the storm. Why? Because *God* can choose to deliver us while we're in the storm or to deliver us out of the storm. Either way, we must be steadfast on the things of *God* by keeping our minds renewed in *God*. When our mind is renewed in *God*, we have this promise from

*God* in the scriptures when we keep our mind stayed on *God*. "Thou wilt keep him in perfect peace, whose mind is stayed on thee" (Isaiah 26:3 KJV).

When we operate in the peace-of-*God* mindset and believe that *God* resides in us, then we can also rest, assured that we have the essence of God himself residing in each of us, which gives us clear indication that *God* never intended for us to do anything in our own power. For we are to rely on *God* for everything, for as the scriptures aptly defines it, our very existence is found in *God* and from *God*.

"For in *him* we live, and move and have our being" (Acts 17:28a KJV). Now, men, because of this fact that our very existence comes from *God*, which dictates how we should live for *God* and counsel with him daily to get our directions from *God*, we have been giving access to the Holy Ghost to guide us in all truth, which is our spiritual compass to move in *God*. As I have mentioned in the previous chapter, in order to know *God*, we must have a relationship with *God*. We must diligently pursue a daily communication with *God*.

All through the Bible, the men of *God*, such as Joseph, Moses, David, Joshua, Paul, Peter, and John and the disciples, walk with the *Lord*. Listen, by no means were they even close to perfection, yet their relationship with *God* was clearly established! Which means they made themselves readily available to be used by *God*. In doing so, they were able to experience the presence of *God* and they were exposed to the essence of *God*.

The essence of *God* will reveal the sovereignty of *God*, which means that *God* still rules. In fact, in the Bible, *God* had to remind King Nebuchadnezzar of this very fact when the *Lord* had to remind him that it was the *Lord* who allowed him to have great wealth and the kingdom to be king. Listen, men, *God* has a way of reminding us who is in charge, as he did with King Nebuchadnezzar. The book of Daniel reveals this chastisement in the Scripture. "The command to leave the stump of the tree with its roots means that your kingdom will be restored to you when you acknowledge that heaven rules" (Daniel 4:26 Life Application Bible Study Bible).

Though the enemy, the devil, may try to wreak havoc in our families, in the country, in our communities, despite all those interferences that the enemy unleashes at us, *God* still reigns. We must do our part—acknowledge that heaven still rules and has the last say! When we don't and when we deliberately reject Christ as *Lord* and Savior, as a man or woman or children of age, to know he is *Lord*, we have accepted Satan as our Father. Listen, make no mistake about it—we're going to have a spiritual father one way or another. Our choice will indicate who our spiritual father will be. Here's what the Bible says about those who reject him as our Father. The Scripture makes it very clear when we reject *God* as *Lord* and Savior over our lives:

> You belong to your Father, the devil, and you want to carry out your Father's desires. He was a murderer from the beginning, not holding to the truth, for there is no truth in Him. When he lies, He speak his native language, for he is a liar and the father of lies. (John 8:44 NIV)

Now on the other hand, the right decision, the only decision that should be made is when we choose *God* as our Father. We begin to see him as a Father, though you may not have an earthly father or if you have an abusive father—then your image of a father may be distorted. The enemy, the devil, will try to distort your view of what a father is to you because of your personal experience or lack thereof from an earthly father.

You see, the enemy's plan is to destroy your image of heavenly Father based on your experiences or lack of with your earthly father. You see, that's the enemy's plan—to destroy your image of your heavenly Father in your mind so that you will choose the devil as your father. But there will come a time when you'll become sick and tired of being sick and tired and you'll come to the end of yourself. Being a sinner is hard work, though you were having much fun in sinning. But look back over your life when you were in the world sinning and doing your thing, the consequences and choices you made in that life. As I mentioned above, the moment you become sick and tired of being sick and tired of the devil's foolishness, you begin to put yourself in a position to be drawn by the Holy Spirit to seek *God*, finding him to now accept him as *Lord* and Savior, once we repented and ask him for forgiveness. The Bible says this when we come to *God* and confess our sins and ask for forgiveness. "If we confess our sins, he is faithful and just and will forgive us our sins and purify us from *all* unrighteousness" (1 John 1:9 NIV).

Now the good news here is, after you decide and chose *God* as your Father, you can begin to reestablish a relationship with *God* that will allow us as men to be led by *God*. In doing so, we begin on the path to discover the essence of *God* simply by your desire to know *God* and really go after *God* fervently. The Bible talks about this fervent attitude, going after *God*. "As the deer pants for streams of water, so my soul pants for you, O *God*, My soul thirst for *God*, for the living *God*" (Psalm 42:1 NIV).

I believe *God* will reveal more of his essence to those of us who go after him more. Now mind you, *God* has no favorites, men. However, if you and I go after him more, especially in a fervent mode, as the Scripture says above, which is to go after *God* with such fervor, and I love how the psalmist David puts it—"as a deer pants for streams of water." Now that deer is really searching for that stream of water as if his very life depends upon it.

This is fervent pursuit—being intentionally persistent, no matter what, like our very lives depends on it, in which it does! Which will allow us to be immersed in his presence, which will reveal the true essence of *God*. Listen, we as men must be in hot pursuit, going after *God* with all our heart and being.

As I mentioned earlier, our very existence can be found in *God*. "For in him we live and move and have our being" (Acts 17:28).

Men of *God*, if we want to operate in our *God*-given authority ordained by *God*, we have to trust and believe the *God* of this universe who created mankind, who created us in his image to represent *God* in the world! We must daily communicate with him. Listen, make no mistake—*God* still speaks to his people today! I can recall an instance when I was driving to work one morning, years ago. While riding to work at around five in the morning, the dawn was breaking just over the horizon. Then it hit me! *God* was speaking in that moment as the early morning sun was beginning to rise. I began shedding tears, and as the tears were rolling down my cheeks as I watched the sunrise, I thought of this scripture in the book of Job. "Have you ever given orders to the morning or shown the dawn it's place" (Job 38:12 NIV). Here in the text, Job is being asked a question by *God*—have you ever given orders to the morning or shown the dawn its place? The depiction here in this text is that every morning, *God* is speaking by giving orders to the morning and telling dawn where to go. I began to realize that I was heading to work in the middle of *God's* conversation to the morning and the dawn. I was sure people on the freeway had no idea why tears were rolling down my cheek if they happened to look inside my car. However, I was witnessing *God*, having conversation with the universe. So listen, next time *God* wakes you up real early in the morning, take a look at the daybreak and witness *God* speaking and giving orders to a new day!

Guess what? It will make you appreciate the scripture, "This is the day that *Lord* has made, let us rejoice and be glad in it." Well, he just spoke it into order, and therefore, it will be a good day because he said so. Men, make no mistake—*God* is still speaking this today. The moment we accept Christ as our *Lord* and Savior, we accept everything that comes with it! We accept his favor, we accept healing, we accept his grace, and we accept his peace, his joy, his love, his authority being imparted to cast out demons! We accept his Word, and we speak that same word with faith and authority over areas of our lives and our families! However, we can only operate in this fashion only by simply obeying the Word of *God*. We obey his Word by knowing the voice of *God*, and we know the voice of *God* by getting into his Word daily. When we do, the scriptures bear witness to the results of the matter. "For his voice becomes clear to each of us. My sheep hear my voice, and I know them and they follow me" (John 10:27 KJV). What a powerful confirmation for each believer, knowing that we know his voice and *God* knows our voice as the scripture just stated. If I may, allow me to unpack what I just wrote.

First, he said that if we're his sheep, that we do hear his voice. Men of *God*, can we grasp that for a moment? We do hear his voice!

Second, Jesus said, "I know them." Third, Jesus said, "And they follow me."

However, men, make no mistake. For this to be reality in our lives, we must make a firm commitment to consume his Word daily. Now I don't want us to gloss over the word *consumed*, which means either "to eat something or to devour as to absorb something." The Bible gives scripture text to back this up. "I fed you with milk and not with solid food; for you were not able to receive it" (1 Corinthians 3:2b NIV). There are growing steps in knowing the Word of *God*, which guides us into knowing *God* personally for ourselves. The scripture indicates that, initially, we're on milk, getting ready for solid food.

I love how Jesus uses this analogy of an infant child who's initially on the mother's milk. However, milk is required for the initial nourishment of our bodies. As we grow into a young child and into a young man, we will begin to progress to the next level of strengthening our natural bodies with meat.

This same analogy must be applied in our spiritual growth with the *Lord*. We must apply ourselves with the Word in getting the basics—the milk—then we grow spiritually into his Word, which is now the meat of the Word, which is establishing a relationship with *God*. In doing so, we now know for sure that we know Jesus and we know that Jesus knows us and hears us! So now, guess what? Exactly, you guessed it! We now follow what we know and what we hear concerning the things of *God*. I once mentioned in one of the previous sermons that I preached that Apostle Paul was chained to the gospel of Christ.

In other word, Paul said this: "For I am not ashamed of the gospel of Christ for it is the power of *God* to Salvation for everyone who believes" (Romans 1:16 NKJV).

As I stated above, going back to the previous sermon analogy of Apostle Paul's bold statement, I said, when we are believers, we are not ashamed of the gospel—we now become forever linked or chained to the gospel. So I alluded to this analogy right here in my sermon: Whatever you are chained to, you will also defend the very thing that you are chained to! Because now, you become sold out to the very thing that you are chained to! If you're chained to the world, you will defend the world and the things of the world. If you're chained or sold out to same-sex marriages, you will defend that thing. If you're chained to fornication, having sex outside of marriage, which is out of the will of *God*—the way *God* intended for us to have sexual relations is in marriage with man and woman only! But if you are chained to having sex outside of marriage, then you will defend that thing. If you believe what *God* says to be true regarding being married before engaging in sexual relationship! Then you and I will defend the very thing we hold to be true, which is the Word of *God*! So just like Apostle Paul boldly proclaimed, he is not ashamed of the gospel of Christ, which means being linked up with Christ. Well, guess what? I'm going to take that same posture or stance the Apostle Paul stood for.

I am not ashamed of the gospel of Christ, which is the power unto salvation. So therefore, I'm going to defend that very thing that I hold to be true, which is the unadulterated Word of *God*! Men of *God*, we defend this thing by having a lifestyle that represents we belong to *God*! Which means, we will always believe and hold fast to the biblical tenets of the scriptures in the Bible and obey the Word of *God* and what the Word of *God* says, which is the standard for holy living in the things of *God*!

We as men must be steadfast in the things of *God*. We can only become steadfast in the things of *God* by purposely consuming the Word of *God* daily. For the Word of *God* is the only substance in which the more we consume it, the hungrier we get. We can never get full on the Word of *God*. In fact, we will develop our spiritual pallet for the Word of *God*, as the scripture bears witness of the spiritual pallet development. "Oh, taste and see that the *Lord* is good; Blessed is the Man who trusts in Him!" (Psalm 34:8 NKJV). Men, by us developing a taste for *God's* Word, we begin to go after *God* with such fervor, which will result in what Scripture says about that. "Therefore my beloved brethren, be steadfast, immovable, always abounding in the work of the *Lord*, knowing that your labor is not in vain in the *Lord*" (1 Corinthians 15:58 KJV). Men, we will become immovable, steadfast, always abounding in the work of the *Lord*. Men of *God*, this is how we get to know *God*—by keeping his Word and obeying his Word at all cost. There is a cost in going after Christ. Here is what Jesus said concerning this matter. "And he said to them all, If anyone desires to come after me, Let him deny himself, and take up his cross and follow me" (Luke 9:23 KJV).

Men of *God*, there is a cost. But here's the good thing about this cost—it was paid for in full on the cross. Yet we must pick up our own spiritual receipt, which is our cross, which is simply denying ourselves and yielding ourselves to the will of *God*. Only then when we yield our will to him that the process of knowing him becomes clear. For it allows us to make him first in our lives. Once again, the Scriptures bears witness of this known truth. "But seek ye first the Kingdom of *God*, and his righteousness, and all these things will be added unto you" (Matthew 6:33). For you see, men, there is a purpose in seeking *God's* kingdom first. Our hearts become yielded unto him, which leads to surrendering life unto *God*. Then *God* will add everything else that we need—even the things that we desire for ourselves will match what *God* desires for us as well. Now what *God* desires for us will be the best for us.

I'm about to say something that will date me. Speaking of my age, how many of you remember the old TV series *Father Knows Best*? Well, guess what? Our heavenly Father definitely knows what is best for us. So, men of *God*, with this being the absolute truth, why wouldn't we totally surrender to the *God* of all creation who created us after his own image? In doing so, he made us to be his answer in the earth to rule under his authority and to rule in that *God*-given authority that he has ordained for us, which was given to us to have dominion over the devil and all his imps, as the Scripture confirms this fact for us. "Behold, I give you the Authority to trample on serpents and scorpions, and over all the Power of the enemy, and nothing shall by any means hurt you" (Luke 10:19 NKJV).

You see, men of *God*, we have to know him and not just need him. In fact, we have to know him—that will give us the grace to know why we need him.

Here is a powerful statement by famous author and evangelist, Pastor Mike Murdock. He once said, "*God* doesn't move in proportion in our lives to how much we need him, but *God* moves in proportion in our lives in how much we know him," which is truly a profound statement because it's absolutely true. We must get to know *God* to operate in *God*!

Listen, when we get to know *God*, the possibilities will be unlimited. For we will now have entered the realm of the supernatural in *God*. Remember, we are spiritual beings created in the image of *God*. We're just housed in a natural body. Yet we have access to the supernatural in *God*. Now ask yourself, how do I know the exact moment we will know him? Well, on this side of heaven, we can't fully know him, as the Scripture confirms this for us. "Now our knowledge is partial and incomplete, and even the gift of prophecy reveals only part of the whole picture" (1 Corinthians 13:9 NLT). Now the scripture makes it plain that our knowledge of him is limited and not complete. But let me assure you that knowing what we know about *God* is more powerful than having the knowledge of the world with all the degrees in the world! We still have this promise from *God* before the foundation of the world—that our authority is in *God*, and from him, there is no ambiguity connected to this promise from *God*, which mean this promise is complete and it can't be broken. As I mentioned earlier, though we know *God* in part, there is a confirmation and promotion from him in scriptures that will give every man who surrender their will to *God's* will. That will give us access to *God* and unlimited knowledge from him. This scripture I will share with you bears repeating in again. So I must share it again. "Henceforth I call you not servants; for the servant knoweth not what his *Lord* doeth: But I have called you friends; for all things that I have heard of my father I have made known unto you" (John 15:15 KJV).

Wow, men! Talking about being in the know, this is truly inside information from the one who is omniscient—the *God* of all knowing. Look at the contrast in both texts in the Bible I just wrote. In the scripture text of 1 Corinthians 13, we only know him in part. In the book of John, it states that if we stay in the process of pursuing *God*, there is an elevation in our pursuit to know *God*.

As the scripture stated, we are no longer servants, for the servants don't know what the master is doing. But now, Jesus makes this profound statement by saying we are now being elevated to a friend of *God*. Jesus goes on to say that everything that his Father tells him, he will turn around and make it known to us! This is truly a remarkable statement by *Jesus*. When we intentionally go after *God* with our entire being, we become connected to the very essence of *God*. Simply by having direct access to *God* with our will aligned to his will, which is the perfect and acceptable will for our lives, which is only accessible by completely surrendering our lives to the will of the Father. When we surrender to the will of the Father, we will then be exposed to more of the essence of *God*. Oftentimes, when there is a disconnection in us experiencing the will of *God*, it is because our view of *God* has now become distorted.

What I mean about our view being distorted is, we think that his will is to send us over to a Third World to do evangelism. However, if that is *God's* call on your life, then he will equip you to do just that. The scriptures will reveal to each of us exactly what his will entails for each born-again believer, which says this, "And be not conformed to this world: But be ye transformed by renewing of your mind, that ye may prove what is the good, and acceptable and perfect will of *God*" (Romans 12:2 KJV).

So what does Scripture say about the perfect will of *God* concerning us? First, our minds must not be attached to the things of the world. Meaning, our minds shouldn't have the world agenda. Our view on how to navigate in this world must be a godly view. For you and I to have a godly view in navigating in this world, we must adhere to what the scripture says. "Let this mind be in you which was in Christ Jesus" (Philippians 2:5 KJV). Once we have a transformed mind, we will have a transformed spirit. We will now have a transformed outlook, which will call us to have a transformed view of the world. Why? Because we now have a transformed mind. Now that our mind is transformed, we can now embrace *God's* acceptable, good, and perfect will for our lives. The moment we embrace *God's* perfect will for our lives, then and only then can we be immersed into his presence that will allow his essence to be witnessed by us.

Once this transformation takes place, we will begin to operate in the things of *God* daily. Why? Because we now have a transformed mind. Then and only then can we now embrace *God's* acceptable and good and perfect will for our lives, men. Wow! Now that's good news, saints! In fact, this is tremendous good news to accept his perfect will for our lives. When we embrace *God's* perfect will for our lives, we will begin to be immersed in his presence that will allow us to be perfect witnesses for the kingdom of *God*. As I mentioned in a previous section, we must familiarize ourselves with the MO of *God*—his method of operation—which will reveal the character of *God*, which will then give us the opportunity to experience the essence of *God*, the very nature of *God*. This book is being written in the time of the pandemic, with the world being shut down by coronavirus, with this being the case with the world being in an upheaval. Now is not the time, men, to shriek back! On the contrary, now is the time more than ever to reacquaint ourselves with *God* with every fiber of our being. We must remove every hindrance that will keep us from going after *God* by repenting and asking *God* for forgiveness and making him priority in our lives. In fact, America must make it a priority to go after *God* with fervent persistence and repentance as well. There are two biblical principles that stand in the Scripture that will corelate with this narrative or mandate, I should say, that will exemplify what it means to fervently go after *God*. "As the deer pants for streams of water, so my soul pants for you, O *God*. My soul thirst for *God*, for the Living *God*" (Psalm 42:1–2 Life Application Study Bible).

Now the scripture, using the word *pant*, gives clear indication of the necessity on how intently this deer is looking for water to quench its thirst. The picture here is that, nothing else will suffice for this deer but water! Well, guess what? We must have that same intensity, men, in our spirit to go after *God* with such fervent urgency, for just like the deer, nothing else will suffice but the living water, which is *God*, that will not only quench our desires for him but also propel us to live in this world and to prepare us to live with him over in glory!

The second scripture that I mentioned is found in the book of Matthew. "But seek first his kingdom and his righteousness, and these things will be given to you as well" (Matthew 6:33 NIV). Now let's unpack these two profound scriptures. The psalmist tells us to go after *God* like our very life depends on it. Guess what? It does! The book of Matthew tells us that there is no other thing in the world that will rival with *God*! Matthew also indicates that in making *God* our priority, it's also like our very lives depend on it. Guess what? It still does. Men, we must pursue *God* in this season because our very lives depend on it. For in the pursuit of *God*, we stay exposed to the essence of *God*. When we stay exposed to the essence of *God*, we will experience the peace of *God*, which will align us to be in the will of *God*.

Listen, men, when we find ourselves in the will of *God*, guess what? Contrary to popular belief regarding the very popular statement, "The happiest place in the world is at Disneyland," well, I'm on the mindset that the happiest place to be for a child of *God* is to be in the will of *God*. Though I like Disneyland very much, I must say the safest place to be for every man, woman, and child is to be in perfect will of *God*. Then and only then can we live a life of fulfilled purpose ordained by *God*.

As I mentioned before, the main component to live in the will of *God* is, we must live a surrendered life to *God*, which requires being obedient to *God*. Men, if we listen and obey the voice of *God*, remember he still speaks today. I believe that in what America and the world is experiencing now because of the coronavirus outbreak that became a pandemic that literally shut down the world as we know it—*God* is speaking now. In fact, he is shouting. What is he shouting? "Hey, America, turn back to me, the maker of heaven and earth." As I mentioned earlier, I'm writing this book in the middle of the coronavirus pandemic, which has claimed the life of a family member to this deadly virus!

So needless to say, it has truly impacted me personally and also made me take inventory of my personal relationship with *God*. So writing this book with the title, *What It Means to Be a Man of God*, well, truly the thought process has changed, not as far as the title of this book but to really look at what it means to be a man of *God*.

I ask myself, where have I fallen short in my role as being a follower of Christ? We know as true believers that America has fallen short. In fact, it is safe to say that America has fallen desperately to the highest order.

We have taken prayer out of the schools. We have gone against the institution of marriage as *God* intended for it to be. Systemic racism has raise its ugly head with senseless murders of Black men and Black women and people of color. We have set up idols contrary to what *God* said—that we shouldn't have any idols before him.

Sin has gone rampant throughout the world. *God* is saying, "Enough is enough." Yet even if we know that America has fallen from grace, we have to take, as individuals, an introspective look within ourselves. So as I am writing this book, I have come to the conclusion that we as men collectively and individually must ask ourselves, have we done what *God* told us to do and have we obeyed him like we should have? In other words, have we been followers of Christ, as what the Word says we should be? Well, let's take a look at what the Scripture says about it. "You are the salt of the earth; but if the salt lose its flavor, how shall it be seasoned? It is good for nothing but to be thrown out and trampled underfoot by men" (Matthew 5:13 NKJV).

Now, men, what does this scripture mean to you on a personal level? Well, let me simplify it for you by unpacking the text. First, men, how do you line up personally on what the scripture said on how we should be as men? What I love about the Word of *God* is he uses simple analogy or parables for us to grasp. Look at the analogy of the word *salt*. What does salt do? Well, it preserves. It adds taste to many food items, especially meat. It also makes one thirsty. So, men, ask yourselves, have you preserved the Word of *God* by studying it and allowing it to mediate in your spirit day and night as *God* told Joshua? Can the world look at you and me and know that we belong to *God*? Have we caused anyone to be thirsty of our lifestyle as men of *God* professing that Christ is King of kings!

The other component of salt is taste. Have we shared with our families, our neighbors, our friends, or in the world? Have we made an indelible imprint in the hearts of people who don't know the Christ we say we love and obey? Well, have you? In exposing them to the Word of *God* to the point of them becoming intrigued enough that we can implore them and say this to them, "O taste and see that the *Lord* is good; Blessed is the man that trusteh in Him" (Psalm 34:8 KJV). Are we doing this, men?

Now the third component is thirst. Are we representing *God* enough in our actions, in our behaviors, in our walk with *God* that is causing people in our families, in our neighborhoods, in our communities, and in the world to be thirsty for the *God* we know and love? If not, men, we have to reevaluate our walk with *God* and get on fire for *God*.

For the church has failed, in my humble opinion, in our responsibility to share the gospel of Christ outside the four walls of the church, with the exception of Love and Unity Christian Fellowship in Compton, California, under the leadership of senior pastor Apostle Ron C. Hill Sr. and co-pastor Lady Osie C. Hill, who have prayed for thousands upon thousands of people being led to Christ, along with Elder Ray Branch and others who I know from firsthand knowledge. This is my church.

So, men, we must embrace our roles more than ever now to represent *God* in this world with more boldness for such a time like this! So let's go after it, men!

Thus far, I have written about getting to know *God* and experiencing the essence of *God* through the Word of *God*. Now in the next section, we will be traveling in the direction to find out *God*'s original plan and purpose for man.

# PART 3

# God's Original
# Purpose for Man

*God's* original purpose for man is to operate in copartnership with *God* the creator—when you think about how *God* created the earth out of nothing by speaking his word in framing the earth, after the creation of earth in all its splendor, beginning with the robust mountains to its majestic seas, the vegetation, and the various plants and array of beautiful flowers and all the animals in the land and in the water.

As the Bible tells us in the book of Genesis, how *God* created all of this beauty called earth. *God* canvassed what he has created and looked upon the vast enormity of his creation. Now, men, I want you to pay close attention on how *God* came to the conclusion in creating mankind. *God* had a board meeting with the Triune of *God* and came to this conclusion: "Let us make man in our image, according to our likeness" (Genesis 1:26 NKJV). Just like any board meeting where plans are being discussed, there is an implementation of plans, which are now being enacted by the board.

So after *God* discussed this with the triune board of heaven to create man in their likeness and in their image, guess what? *God* implemented what they agreed to do. And the Scripture bears witness to this fact. "So *God* created Men in his own image; in the image of *God* he created him; male and female he created them" (Genesis 1:27 NKJV).

Now remember when I stated that *God's* original purpose for man was to be in copartnership with *God* in managing the earth and everything in it, which *God* had created. This statement I'm going to share with you now confirms the fact about how we were created to be in copartnership with *God*.

"Out of the ground the *Lord* formed every beast of the field and every bird of the Air, and brought them to Adam to see what he would call each living creatures their name" (Genesis 2:19 NKJV).

Now think about what *God* entrusted in Adam's care, think about this for a moment—every animal that exists (the different shapes, the different sizes, the different-looking animals) from the smallest, such as an ant, to the largest size, such as the gorilla and the elephant. Then in the waters, from the smallest fish to the killer whales. Yet Adam just looked upon each animal and just named each one of them as he saw them, and *God* accepted everything that Adam had named.

The evidence of these scriptures clearly shows how the creator of mankind, *God* himself, partnered with Adam in allowing him to name what *God* has created. Men, that's some powerful stuff right there!

There was a very distinct connection between *God* the creator and his creation, man. The connection between *God* and man was so in sync to the point that, every evening, *God* met up with Adam to talk over what Adam did throughout the day. Well, guess what, men? *God* is still interested with each of us, to talk to us concerning our day.

Now mind you, because he is *God*, he already knew what Adam was doing, just like he knows everything that we're doing. *God* just enjoyed the relationship he had with Adam, and he enjoys the relationship he has with us who have surrendered to his will. Henceforth, this is what *God's* original purpose for man is—to get back in having a personal relationship with him and get back in copartnership with *God* as he intended man's role to be in the earth before the foundation of the world.

However, this relationship was severe when Adam disobeyed *God*, as is the case today, men, when we disobey *God*. Adam was given a direct order by *God*, which was not to touch the one tree in the garden. Yet Adam had access to everything else that *God* had created. Adam's sole position was to manage the universe under the guidance and the authority given to him by *God*. In conjunction with what *God* commanded Adam to do as I have stated, he and Adam met every evening in the cool of day because of the relationship they had. Yet *God* looked upon Adam and saw something missing. So *God*, in his infinite wisdom and mercy and grace, looked upon all his creation and saw every creature that he had made and the female counterpart for each creation. Then *God* looked upon Adam and decided that the male Adam needed a female counterpart as well. *God* decided that Adam needed a helpmate.

> And the *Lord God* caused a deep sleep to fall on Adam, and he slept; and he took one of his ribs, and closed up the flesh in its place. Then the rib which the *Lord God* had taken from the man he made into a Woman and he brought her to man. (Genesis 2:21–22 NKJV)

Now, once *God* brought Adam his helpmate to him, *God* still gave him the responsibility of naming what he had just created. Now Adam, being true to his form, called his helpmate the correct name, which is woman. Now, Adam has a helpmate—a beautiful woman to assist in managing *God's* creation.

*God's* original purpose and orders now that Adam has his helpmate was still intact. The order to Adam was still the same—"do not eat of this particular tree." But as I said, everything else Adam has access to and still keep his partnership assignment with *God* intact. Men, even today, when we have been given an assignment by *God*, it can never be compromised, even in marriage. We have to trust what *God* told us—that he will give our wives peace and understanding in complying with the will of *God*.

Now *God* gave them both purposes and assignments to do and complete in *God's* creation. The Scripture bears witness to this fact as well. "Then *God* blessed them, and *God* said to them, Be fruitful and Multiply; fill the earth and subdue it; Have dominion over the fish of the sea, over the birds of the air, and over every living thing that moves on the earth" (Genesis 1:28 NKJV).

The plans of *God* that he had created for mankind remain intact for us today, even after the fall of the first Adam. *God* gave them direct command to subdue the earth and multiply in the universe. Now that Adam had his helpmate and the blessings of *God* was upon them, at this point, all they had to do was to fulfill their roles as manager and co-manager of *God's* creation and subdue and multiply in the earth. Well, that same mandate is given to the married couples today who profess and confess that the *Lord* is their *Lord* and *Savior*. If we comply with what *God* said to us just like he said to Adam and Eve. But there was an interruption in the plans if you may, meaning that Satan had raised up to tempt Eve, which God knew. *God* knew that the serpent Satan was going to tempt Eve. But the order was given to Adam not to touch the forbidden fruit was a direct command to Adam by *God*. As I mentioned earlier, even today in our Christian marriages, there are things that *God* has commanded the husband to do or not to do—and it must never be compromised.

So Eve could have eaten the whole tree and nothing would of happen to them. Why? Because the command was given to Adam. But Adam was right there when his wife decided to partake of the forbidden tree. Then she offered her husband, Adam, the fruit, and of course, we know that Adam ate the fruit, and we all know what transpired. The blame game began to take root. Guilt got introduced, followed by shame, which caused them both to run away from *God*, instead of running to *God* even after they failed. As they were hiding from *God*, they heard the voice of *God* asking this question which was recorded in the Bible. The scripture says this: "But the *Lord God* called to Man, Where are You?" (Genesis 3:9 NIV).

Well, guess what, men? *God* is still asking that same question today to all men who profess to know Christ as *Lord* and Savior. *God* is asking, "Man, where are you?" You see, *God's* original purpose for man still remains today as it was in the beginning, which is for man and his woman (wife) in a covenant marriage to subdue and multiply in the earth, as I mentioned, even with the fall of the first Adam, which brought sin into this world through the manipulation of the serpent the devil, which is still manipulating the world today.

But *God* has a plan to reconcile man back to him through the second Adam, who is Jesus Christ, who died for the sins of the world and went into the depths of the earth to take the keys back from Satan, which Adam relinquished when he fell from grace. Christ defeated death and arose with all power to reconcile man back to *God*.

Yet because of free will, we have the option to choose Christ as our *Lord* and Savior. This gave us all the opportunity, men, to fulfill our mandate of his commandment, which he gave to the first Adam. As I mentioned before, *God* is still asking this question to men, "Where are you?"

There is work that we as men of *God* must do. For us to do this work, we must be kingdom-minded, which is to get involved in *God's* business, which is saving souls by sharing the gospel of Jesus Christ. We do this by the same two criteria that *God* gave Adam, which is to subdue the earth and multiply in the earth, yet the mission is different in regard to what we subdue and what we are to multiply.

Here's the difference—in the Garden of Eden, the command on what to subdue and multiply was different. Remember, the world was perfect and *God* gave them everything and their sole responsibility was to govern what *God* has created. And to fill the earth with its seed, to multiply the human race, to give birth more managers to help govern and increase in the earth.

Now for us in today's world, our command to subdue is to bring down the kingdom of darkness and multiply the army of *God* by making disciples by sharing the gospel of Christ to the world. In other words, men of *God*, we are still *God's* answers in the world, which is to bring the gospel of Christ to the dying world. However, for us as men to operate in our ordained assignment to be *God's* answer in this world, we have to operate in the capacity, as I mentioned earlier in this book, which is—we must be the salt and light of the world. As I mentioned, the purpose of being salt is to preserve the tenets of the gospel by not only being hearers of the Word of *God* but we must be doers of the Word of *God*. We do this by implementing the Word of *God* in action, by doing what thus says the *Lord*, which is to become the salt and light in the world.

The acronym I have for SALT is *S*anctified, *A*nointed, *L*oving, *T*riumphant. No doubt, if we represent holy salt, we will truly illuminate the world by being the light in the world amongst all the darkness. We have the concept all wrong in our depiction of darkness. I use this analogy when walking in a dark room. We often say it's dark inside there; in fact, darkness is saying, "Oh no! Here comes *light*!" You see, darkness has no defense when light enters the room. Once the light switch is turned on, darkness must go! For we have been equipped to activate that light in us when darkness raises its ugly head. The Scripture bears witness that we have been equipped by Christ. "I can do all things through Christ which strengtheneth me" (Philippians 4:13 KJV).

Now, men, because of this scripture, we can also hang our hat on this scripture as well. This powerful scripture of validation is confirmed in us when we operate in the things of *God*. In the book of 2 Corinthians 2:14a (KJV), "Now thanks be unto *God*, which always causeth us to triumph in Christ."

Men, did you catch a hold of this profound statement by the apostle Paul? Allow me to play back for you again in writing: "Now thanks be unto *God* which always causeth us to triumphant in Christ!"

Men, did you hear the word *always*, which means "every time, on every occasion, without exception." Men, when we operate in Christ, we can boldly say these words to this song I remember singing in church growing up. Remember this song, "Victory is mine, Victory is mine, Victory today is mine, I told satan to get thee behind me, Victory today is Mines!" (Dorothy Norwood).

However, according to the scripture, victory is not only today! But always, we will triumphant and have daily victories because of

Christ. So, men, with this absolute promise we have from *God* that victory is eminent in every area of our lives, even in the moments in our lives when we face our darkest moments, we still have the victory. Yet I know each man reading this book can relate to experiencing some dark moments in your lives.

But *God* says to us that because of him, he will always cause us to triumph, even when we can't see it when the dark moments are thrusted upon us. There is a scripture in the book of Deuteronomy that speaks on another promise, always, to us by *God*. "The *Lord* will make you the head, not the tail, if you pay attention to the commands of the *Lord* your *God* that I give you this day and carefully follow them. You will *always* be on top, never at the bottom" (Deuteronomy 28:13).

Now listen, initially, when reading this text and taking it on its face value, remember all the scriptures are inspired by *God*. In reading this text, we can get really happy about being *always* on top and never at the bottom. Yet we know that there are times in our lives when those dark moments I mentioned earlier come upon us. That we don't feel in those moments that we're *always* on top and you will never be on the bottom. In fact, on the contrary, in those moments, we feel like we just hit rock bottom in those dark moments in our lives.

But *God* makes this bold proclamation that we are never at the bottom! Because we're always on top! I can hear you saying right now, "But, *God*, how am I on top of this situation, this moment in my life, when I'm facing this profound tragedy in my life?" Yet *God* said we're always on top and never at the bottom. Our response may be, "Well, *Lord*, it sure doesn't look like it or feel like it."

Then I'm reminded of what the Scripture says. "And we know that in all things *God* works for the good of those love him, who have been called according to his purpose" (Romans 8:28 NIV). When the scripture says *all things*, it means that the sovereignty of *God* can take all the bad things and the good things and the almost things to work it for our good, not that it was good to us or for us. But *God* can use the darkest moments in our lives to become bright moments in our lives. *God* can turn our desert experiences into a Living Waters of Paradise.

So, men, with this being the case, what do we do when *God* says we're always on top and never at the bottom? Well, here is what we do. We go to examine the scriptures to examine how *God* can make such a bold statement like that.

The Scripture says in Deuteronomy, "If we pay attention to the commands of the *Lord* your *God* that I give you this day and carefully follow them." Now wait for it, we will always be on top and never at the bottom. Men, here's the recap—*God* says all things work together for our good. If we want to experience the truth and the fullness of his Word, that tells you and me and every Christian that we will always be on top and never at the bottom, even in our darkest moments.

First, we must pay close attention to every word that *God* has said in his Word. Second, we must apply the Word of *God* to every area of our lives. We must allow the *Lord* to be our Savior and our Master. Third, when we fulfil the first two components, then we will experience being on top and never at the bottom, even in the darkest moments of our lives. Though we may not fully grasp this, yet we may know this to be true and yet not fully understand it and come to the realization that *God* is sovereign and he knows what he is doing and when to do it and how to release it, even when we just don't understand!

I can recall a personal moment to what I stated before, that we all have experienced some painful moments in our lives to call us to question *God*.

I had a such a moment in my life when my mother transitioned into the presence of the *Lord*. My mother, Evangelist Mary L. Thomas, and I were very close. My mother saw me getting ordained into eldership in the Church of *God* in Christ by my former pastor, Bishop E. G. Mclachlan. My mother saw me preach my first sermon. My mother asked me to eulogize her husband, my father, Marion J. Thomas Sr., who is also resting in the presence of the *Lord*. So when my mother became sick, I asked *God* to heal my mother and bring her home.

Well, *God* ultimately healed her completely and brought her home. But it wasn't the home that I was talking about. Because he took my mother to the home he prepared for her instead. I can still recall that day so vividly, on August 2, 2012. When I heard the hospital page code blue and my mother's doctor being called back to my mother's room. I had just left my mother's room after conferring with the doctor and was heading to the cafeteria to get water. I just called the rest of my family and shared with them that Mom was okay and doing well. Yet, I found myself rushing down the hallway back to my mother's room. Even now, I get teary-eyed, though I know she's in the presence of the *Lord*.

When I got back to my mother's room, they were trying to resuscitate her. The staff that day were all my mother's favorites, for they were all saved, who confessed Christ with wonderful personalities and bedside manners. As I look back on that day, even *God* orchestrated that. Remember when I said all things works to the good for those who love Christ?

My mother knew how to draw people to her, or should I say that people were drawn to my mother. As I was saying, my mother was being worked on by her doctor, and I was praying hard for my mother, crying out to *God*! Then I glanced over toward her face, and there was a glow. Then I heard the doctor say, "I feel a heartbeat," but like I said, I saw a glow on my mother's face.

Then the *Lord* spoke to me and said, "Your mother, my daughter in Zion, was having an apostle Paul type of moment." My mother was betwixt. She knew we/I still need her. My mother also knew it was far better to be with Christ! Now as I am writing this, it's becoming clear to me that *God* simply obeyed my mother's wishes. Yet at that moment, I question *God* why!

When he had already revealed to me why, the far better was at hand! At that moment, seeing my mother transitioning to be with the *Lord*, my whole life changed. I remember that day so vividly— the sky was bluer, the birds were chirping crystal clear to my ears; definitely my senses were heightened.

It seemed like the world stood still as my mother was making her entrance into being in the presence of the *Lord*. Though I knew she was in his presence, I was very upset with *God* because I asked him to bring her home. Well, he did just that—to his home, not the home where my mother raised all of her three children (me; my sister, Denise Lynn Powell; and my brother, Darrell Wayne Thomas).

So when I look back on that moment, I cannot say it was a dark moment, though it felt like it because I didn't have my mother. Yet the reality was I had my mother for eighty-two years of her life and my dad for ninety-one years of his life, and they are now both in the presence of the *Lord*. I'm blessed beyond measure actually, and the *Lord* has graced me to do both of my parents' eulogy, which *God* gave me the strength and the fortitude along with his anointing to do what he ordained me to do before the foundation of the world. So *God's* purpose for me was still on track for my life, even though at that time, it sure didn't feel like it.

Though we face different challenges in our lives, men, *God's* original purposes for our lives can never be altered—delayed yes, but never altered!

In fact, *God* original purpose for each of our lives begins at birth. The moment *God* breathed life into us, our purpose was instilled in our DNA from the beginning. Now, I can almost hear you saying, "How do I know what my purpose is?" Well, if you really want to find your true purpose in life, then you and I must go to the one who created us and put purpose inside of us.

Our individual relationship with *God* will bring our purpose to the forefront to be honed and perfected by *God*. However, we must not confuse what our purpose is and what *God's* original purpose for our lives is. Now I hear you saying, "What do you mean?" Well, let me break it down for you. We all have gifts and talents embedded in each of us at conception of birth, as I stated earlier. One of the ways we recognize our gifts and talents is whatever we like doing, it flows from you with little effort; as opposed to when someone operates outside their gift, it requires a great deal of effort. However, when we operate in our gifts, it is effortless and you will enjoy what you're doing to the point that money is not really an issue. Why? Because we're operating in our wheelhouse—a baseball term that means you're operating in a position to be put in the best possible place to be in life. In fact, the Scripture makes it clear that we don't have to flaunt our gift—it will make room for you. "A man's gift makes room for him, And bringeth him before great men" (Proverbs 18:16 KJV).

Which authorized our gifts to be recognized by others, which will bring glory to the giver of our gifts and not to us. In fact, *God* wants us to be successful his way, which will cause us to be prosperous by him. But first, we must do this: "But seek ye first the Kingdom of *God*, and his righteousness; and all these things shall be added unto you" (Matthew 6:33 KJV).

There you have it—we must seek the kingdom of *God* first. That is *God's* original plan for our lives, men. In the kingdom, we are equipped with the things of *God* to go forth in this world to represent Christ by sharing the gospel to the lost. We are to create a culture of discipleship by operating in the kingdom principles of *God*. We do that by establishing a relationship with *God* by spending purposeful time reading the Word of *God* and by fasting and praying.

When we apply these three essential spiritual ingredients in our spiritual arsenal, we put ourselves in a position to receive *God's* best for us. In fact, the scripture that comes to mind to summarize the challenges we will face in life, even our most greatest challenges in life, *God's* sovereignty is still on display in our lives through the pain and challenges. As the Scripture indicates, "And we know that all things work together for good the to those who love *God*, to those who are the called according to His purpose" (Romans 8:28 NKJV).

Now the scripture is not saying all things that happen to us are good things. But all things work together for our good according to his purpose. Whoever *God* has called, he has also qualified.

With that being the case, our purpose in *God* is still on trac and *God's* original purpose for each of us who obey and align with his will. Our purpose will never be forfeited regarding our lives, men. For the Word of *God* confirms this as well. "I know that you can do all things and that no plans of Yours can be thwarted" (Job 42:2 NIV). So, men, in other words, no matter what we do in this life! *God's* purpose cannot be aborted or thwarted.

When I look up the word *thwart*, the meaning is "to hinder." In other words, *God's* plans for us will always come to pass! No matter what!

So with that being the case, we can take great solace in the fact that no matter the challenges we face and the obstacles we will encounter, it doesn't matter. No matter how hopeless we may think our situation is, no matter how bleak the circumstances of our current situation may look like, the fact of the matter is, *God's* plans for us will not, never, ever will fail. The Scripture bears witness of this fact concerning *God's* plan for our lives. "For I know the plans I have for you, declares the *Lord*, plans to prosper you and not to harm you, plans to give you hope and a future" (Jeremiah 29:11 NIV).

So once again, *God's* plans for us will not fail. If you noticed in the scriptures, *God* has more than one plan. I ventured to say that each plan will take us into a higher level with *God*.

His will is for us to come into conformity concerning his prefect will for our lives as men of *God*, to facilitate his gospel throughout the world.

When we align ourselves with his will by being obedient to his Word and continuing to communicate with him by prayer, fasting, and daily communing with the Holy Spirit, then we will begin to see the purpose and plans for our lives unfolding and coming to fruition right before our eyes.

Then what we have been ordained to do for *God*, it will become a joyous experience to be in our purpose and to be in the will of *God*. For we were created just for that—orchestrated and ordained by *God*.

The Scripture bears witness to this fact as well. "For we are *God's* Masterpiece he has created us anew in Christ Jesus, so we can do the good things he planned for us long ago" (Ephesians 2:10 NLT).

Wow! Look at this, men. At birth, *God* imparted in us everything we need to be successful. Plus, he called us his masterpiece, being created in his image. So with that being the case, we have been equipped to do great things through *God*, not that we are great but we serve a great *God* who has ordained us from birth to do good works through him and by him.

With that being established by *God* from birth, we can take great solace of the fact that we have been authorized by *God* in fulfilling our purpose through *God*.

Our relationship with *God* is the key in fulfilling *God's* original purpose for our lives. As I mentioned before in the previous sections of the book, we establish our intimate relationship with *God* by being communicable in prayer and by digesting his Word daily. Listen, men, when we commit ourselves in doing what I just wrote, we will find out through the Word of *God* what *God* wants, what *God* needs, what *God* has commanded. So when we obey his Word, we align ourselves to be conformed to his will for our lives.

When we establish those criteria by reading and studying the Word of *God*, then our desires will be to do his bidding in the earth. Remember, we are not only *God's* masterpieces, we are also called to be spiritual fisherman of mankind, sharing the gospel of Christ to a fallen world.

Though some will reject him, that's not our problem, though it will be a concern those who willfully reject the message of the gospel. We are just conduits, all yielded vessels, by which *God* will use to share this powerful gospel first in our families, in our neighborhoods, in our cities, in our state, in our country, throughout the world. *God* has already given us everything we need to be successful in life.

We have been blessed with every spiritual blessing, and we have been seated with Christ in heavenly places. We have the Holy Spirit to guide us in all truth.

Our position in Christ has been solidified from birth, though there was a disconnection when sin came into the world. But thank *God* for his son, Jesus Christ, who died on Calvary for our sins, which afforded each of us with the opportunity to accept him as our *Lord* and Savior to be reconciled back to *God*. That has reestablished our connection back to *God*.

Now that we have been reconciled back to *God*, we are now on trac to fulfill our *God*-given destiny established by him from the beginning of time.

In fact, with truth being told, there is a void that we feel as men when we are not operating in our natural purpose, which is to be a provider and a protector, as well as a teacher. These roles define each of us as men. I believe these roles were instilled in us from birth. When we find ourselves, at times, for whatever reason, not in the position to operate in the capacity of protector, provider, and teacher, we feel an empty void within ourselves, even when we're not in the position to operate in this capacity through no fault of our own, because this was imputed in us at birth as men in creation. For *God* put that ability in every man to be a provider and protector and teacher. However, when we operate apart from *God*, we will fail. *God* set the order by which these gifts are to be operated in. Here is the order that *God* will have us to follow: "But I would have you know, that the head of everyman is Christ; and the head of the woman is Man; and the head of Christ is *God*" (1 Corinthians 11:3 NIV/KJV).

There is a distinct order *God* has designed for all men to follow once we profess that *God* is our *Lord* and *Savior*. He designed this order, and it cannot be altered, even when we as men don't feel like we can't operate in this capacity because of a lack of financial stability. Therefore, we can't protect, and therefore, we can't teach. Yet when we seek a divine, intimate relationship with *God*, we will fill our roles as *God* has laid it out for us. Now Scripture indicates these roles to be activated in a godly marriage between man and woman. These particular roles can only be carried out in a marriage. But these roles can also be implemented in being single as well, with *God* and Christ being the lead, until we find a helpmate. Either way, we must be doers of the Word and not just hearers of the Word only. Also, the wife must be a believer of the gospel of Christ as well. We are to be equally yoked so we can be aligned for discipleship in the Word of *God*. This is why the Bible implores us not to be unequally yoked so we can be on the right path of the marriage. So being married to your wife is only part of the equation. The other part of the equation is that we both must be Christians and each of us should have our personal relationship with *God*, as I stated above. Why is this so important in a marriage? Because there will be times in the marriage when *God* speaks to the husband's helpmate, the wife, especially when the husband keeps missing the voice of *God*. Because for whatever reason, he has allowed interference to come between his signals and *God's* signals. That's why the husband is blessed with a wife who loves the *Lord* and who is his helpmate. Remember, the Scriptures says, "He who finds a wife, Finds Favor with the *Lord*."

Remember I just said that the husband's signal is blocked from hearing from the *Lord*. Well, remember, the husband's role should be of godly leadership and not fleshly dictatorship, then he will hear from the *Lord*. For when the husband operates in the capacity of godly leadership, it is for the godly wife to follow her godly husband. However, when the husband is behaving ungodly and causing grief to his wife, the weaker vessel, according the scripture, when this happens, the prayers of the husband will not leave the room—it will just bounce off the ceiling walls. When this happens, the wife must stay in the order of relationship as *God* has decreed. But if there is physical violence, verbal abuse, then, of course, by all means, the wife should seek shelter. But if it's just disagreements without violence and the husband is just being stubborn or hardheaded as we used to say, if the wife stays put in the order of *God* as he has designed it, then she will begin to pray for her husband—that *God* will change the heart of the husband. But the moment the wife steps out of the godly order and confides in friends and other family members, then *God* cannot move on her behalf.

*God* will not honor either position when we operate outside the will and the order of *God* inside the marriage. Like I just said, if the wife stays in compliance with *God's* order for the marriage, then *God* will bring that husband or that wife back in order of his way, not our ways.

It's the very reason *God* set it up this way so we can have total reliance on *God* and in him alone. *God* can only move in this direction when we both operate in faith and being totally reliant on him. This is the order that *God* has set up, which is the order of family and purpose that applies to the husband and the wife. So as men, this protocol was instilled in us at birth, even as a single man dating in a relationship with a woman. We still have the propensity to lead, provide, and teach. Why? Because *God* has put this in us and we may have also witnessed this by our fathers and mothers.

56

However, if we're not committed in serving and obeying Christ as Christians, being followers of Christ, we will never be able to operate in that godly order without establishing a relationship with Christ by accepting him as *Lord* and Savior of our lives.

Which is *God's* original purpose for our lives to begin with. During the pandemic season of COVID-19, we all became reacquainted with a word that we may not recall using before this pandemic. The word *essential* was a constant in our vocabulary. Well, there is nothing more essential than our salvation in Christ, along with having a personal, intimate relationship with the creator of mankind.

Only then and only then can we fulfill our *God*-given purpose assigned to us by *God*. When you think about being in a relationship and what is required to maintain the relationship, the effort and sacrifices one has to make as man and woman that may develop into a fiancé relationship that will lead to marriage.

The commitment level reaches new heights and different parameters that will allow each person to fulfill their roles in the relationship to keep the marriage strong and vibrant—for the roles have now completely changed, especially for the man, for now, he has been commanded by *God* to love his wife like Christ loves the church.

The wife's role is to submit to her husband and honor him and reverence him. Now I'm not writing a book on marriages. I know some of you may be saying, "Let me look at the book cover again, for I thought the title was *What It Means to Be a Man of God.*" Or you may be wondering about the message shift. Well, let me assure you the message hasn't shifted. I just wanted to refer to the different nuisance of being in a committed relationship and the work it takes to make it work.

But being in a relationship with *God* requires us to totally surrender if we will have any chance to fulfill our roles, men, as a husband to a wife. Men, when we surrender to *God*, he will lead us to an abundant life more than we can think or imagine.

In fact, the Scripture verifies this for us, men. "Now unto Him that is able to do exceeding abundantly above all that we ask or think, according to the power that worketh in us" (Ephesians 3:20 KJV).

Men, *God* wants to release his blessings on us so much that his heart aches to do just that. However, *God* wants to be able trust what he entrusted to us, so we must be totally depending on *God*, as I mentioned earlier in the book—that we must be like deer panting for the water brooks as the psalmist wrote for us in the book of Psalms.

*God* meant what he said when he asked us to give all of our concerns, all of our problems to him. Yet this walk with *God* requires complete faith in him. We can only learn this kind of faith by walking with *God*, to have a life totally dependent on *God*, knowing that he can't fail. Yet when hardships of life come upon us and we don't understand why, we trust *God* in the pain and through the pain, for we know that *God* doesn't make any mistakes. However, while we're going through it, we can't see the hands of *God* moving in our direction, yet knowing that he promised to never leave us nor forsake us. When we have to come to the same conclusion that Job came to in the book of Job when he didn't see the hands of *God* being visible:

> But Job said this, Behold, I go forward, but he is not there; and backward, but I cannot perceive Him:
> On the left hand, where he doth work, but I cannot behold him: He hideth himself on the right hand, that I cannot see him: *But he knoweth the way that I take: When He hath tried me I shall come forth as Gold.* (Job 23:8–10 KJV)

Now, men, let me break this down for us. Job gave his account on what it is not knowing where *God* is or not hearing from *God* in our struggles, going through the trials of life without feeling the presence of *God* in our struggles.

Well, can I get a show of hands of how many of you out there has experienced what Job experienced? I see you, guys, hands up. Brothers, keep your hands up so *God* can see you.

Guess what? My hand is up too! Listen, *God* will not always appear when we want him too or according to the way we think he should appear or not even according to how he appeared before. In these scriptures I just gave, Job made an interesting observation concerning *God's* previous deliverances that he had experienced.

Job said, "On my left hand where you did work, I didn't see you on that side anymore! Where are you, *God?*"

That same question was being asked during the pandemic season of COVID-19. Where are you, *God?* Listen, when we fully surrender to *God*, as I mentioned before, and totally trust *God*, often times, if not most of the time, *God* does not fill in the blanks on how he will deliver us out of our current troubles.

Yet just like Job who couldn't trace his presence, just like we can't trace the presence of *God* in our times of crisis, though we can't trace his presence, his heart is traceable! But we know his heart, which says that he will never leave us nor forsake us! That's his heart! So we must come to the same conclusion that Job came to in verse 10, where Job boldly stated, "*But he knoweth the way* I take." The *Lord* knows the way we should go, men. For *God* knows what is best for you and me. We're not supposed to figure *God* out, but trust him in the process, men."

Sometimes, *God* will keep us in a situation and choose to deliver us in the situation as opposed to delivering us out of the situation because he is *God* and *God* all by himself. Those are the times when *God* is trying to grow us, just like Job said in the text. "He hath tried me I *shall* come forth as Gold."

Yes, *God* loves us so much that he wants to grow us, prune us, as job said—"that we come out like pure gold."

Men, because *God* is an all-knowing *God*, he sees things in our future that we can't begin to see. He sees the storms, he sees the obstacles on the horizon, the unexpected hurts and pains for us but not unexpected to him. But to us, he has tried us so we can come out like pure gold.

In other words, there is some purging and pruning that needs to be done in our lives so that we can face the future storms with the full assurance that we can trust *God* through it all.

So, men, when we fully encounter *God* by having an intimate relationship with him, when we go through trials, we know that *God* is with us. Even if we can't trace his presence, we can always trace his heart. Because we know his heart through the scriptures and by having an intimate relationship with him. We know he will never leave us nor forsake us! We can now go through life knowing that we are operating in *God's* original purpose for our lives, which is to be fishers of men by promoting the gospel and going after *God* like the deer panting for the water brooks as the scripture has stated.

We will walk in our purpose. In the next section, we will explore what it means to be created in his image and to reflect that lifestyle on earth. I'm excited about this! How about you?

# PART 4

# What It Means to Be Created in the Image of God

When you think about what it means to be created in the image of *God*, first, one must come to grips with the fact that we were fashioned after his own image—the image of *God*.

It's truly mind-boggling to get our minds wrapped around the fact of being created in the image of the living *God*! For when we look at society at large, we are made from different ethnicity. We are different races, different sizes, different languages. We are different physically in every way; we are males and females.

Yet *God* has boldly stated in his Word that we are created in his image as the scriptures has stated. "And *God* said, Let us make man in our image, after our likeness" (Genesis 1:26A KJV). So let's take a look at the context of this scripture so that we can get a better understanding of what it means to be created in the image of the true, living *God*.

The scripture indicates that we were created in his image and likeness. Now mind you, no one has ever seen *God*. So the question can be asked—how do we see ourselves as men and women in his image when there is no image of him to see? How can we know what his image is if we have no physical image of him?

Well, the Scripture gives us a clue on how we can do just that. We were created in his image and, wait for it, his likeness. What is his likeness? Can it be a representation of his image? So since we all look differently physically, how can we all be created in his image? Well, the only way for you and me to portray his image and his likeness is we must first find out what *God* is like.

We find out what *God* is like by spending dedicated time in reading his Word and studying his Word. As I just stated, when we purposefully and willingly spend time in his Word and have active prayer life, as well as fasting before the *Lord*, then we will begin to conform to his likeness and his image by being in the Word of *God*, which is alive and active and sharp as a two-edged sword, as the Bible tells us.

The Word will begin to reveal *God* to you. That's why before we begin to read his Word, we should ask the Holy Spirit to reveal what *God* is saying in his Word personally to you. *God* will do just that—reveal himself to you through his Word. Then you and I will begin to conform in his image and his likeness because the Word of *God* is a revealer of who he is and who we are in him.

The Scriptures bears witness to this fact in conforming to his image. "For whom he did foreknew, He also predestined to be conformed to the image of His Son" (Romans 8: 29a KJV).

We conformed, as I stated, by reading and obeying his Word, then living it out on the earth by being living epistles as Apostle Paul wrote in the Bible, stating that we are being read by all men.

Our lifestyle should reflect the very tenets of the nature of *God*. What is the nature of *God*? Remember we explored that in the beginning section of the book.

*God* is love, he is kind, he is merciful and gracious. When we reflect these attributes of *God*, we're reflecting the image and likeness of *God*.

The Scripture reminds us that we are supposed to be living epistles being read by all men. "You show that you are our letter, written on our hearts, known and read by everybody" (2 Corinthians 3:2 NIV).

So listen, if we as men are supposed to be read by everybody, then we should give them something to read about. We can never live above where we're at regarding to Word of *God*. So it behooves us to get into the Word of *God* daily by being doers of the Word and not just hearers of Word. Then we can find out what *God* is like and begin to emulate those traits in our lives daily. Often times, when I preach before *God's* people, I often say, as I prepare to give *God's* Word, that they see Christ and not the minister.

Our talk, our walk, our actions must reflect the likeness of Christ. We don't approach life with the lenses of the world; on the contrary, we approach life by the lenses of Christ.

What does Christ see? He sees opportunities for us to serve, not to be served. This serving starts in our families.

If our families don't see Christ operating in our lives in the home—before the world reads us, the best read should begin in our homes where the family resides. If it doesn't begin there, then how can we effectively operate in our calling in the public eye? If we can't effectively display Christ-like behavior in our homes, then our ministry becomes watered down at best with no real power.

We may think we have godly attributes. But the facts will reveal otherwise in our behavior and actions in our homes, as opposed to our walk with the masses.

In other words, we become delusional in our walk with *God*. Because our families are our greatest ministry. When Jesus told his disciples this after they got filled with the Holy Spirit., they became effective witnesses in the world.

> But Jesus admonishment to his disciples in terms where he wanted them to start their ministry of reconciliation… And ye shall be witnesses unto me both in Jerusalem and in all Judaea, and in Samaria and unto the uttermost part of the earth. (Acts 1:8b KJV)

Here in the text, Jesus made it clear where to start the ministry of reconciliation. Its starts in Jerusalem! Yes, it starts at home first!

We must become effective communicators of the love of Christ and the joy and peace it gives us when we lead a surrendered life in *God*. Listen, the message must be first displayed in our homes.

Jesus knew how important it is for us to begin our ministry in our homes. Oftentimes, families of pastor, the children in these homes, feel left out of the equation of being loved like Christ loves the church because the pastors of those families didn't find the balance between the church and their personal lives, which is their families. In those instances, the pastors have not engaged with *God* for wisdom in order for them to navigate the ministry to be effective at home first and then the church. If the pastors of these families don't consult with *God*, then children of those families will feel left out and oftentimes grow up rebellious. But there are exceptions to the rule. There are pastoral families where children see the same love amongst them as they see in the church. Then the children of those families become attracted to the ministry and the love of Christ. They themselves become effective witnesses of the gospel themselves by emulating their parents in the ministry. So, men of *God*, we must exemplify these same traits within our families.

When we operate in the image and likeness of *God*, then we become fully engaged with our families and outside the four walls of the church, the families in the world. When we operate in the love of Christ, we show the world the likeness of Christ, and when we show the likeness of Christ, we will then begin to mirror the image of *God* to the lost and the dying world who desperately needs a savior like we did! The Scripture bears witness to this known fact. We are to imitate Christ as the Bible tells us that's who we are. "Therefore be imitators of *God* as dear children, And walk in love, as Christ also loved us" (Ephesians 5:1 NKJV).

So, men, we are called to be imitators of Christ, and the Bible clearly outlines this for us to follow. We do what Christ does, which is to operate in love. These are the images of *God* that we are to display in our lives as men to show the world that we belong to *God*.

When we display the main attribute of *God*, which is love, we will reveal to others we belong to *God*. The Scripture verifies this fact for us as well. "By this shall all men know that you are my disciples if you have love for one another" (John 13:35 NKJV). There must be a continual flow of *God*'s love emulating from us toward humanity. Now for this to be personified in our lives, men, we must stay connected to our life source, who is Christ Jesus our *Lord* and Savior. For he is the fountain of love, peace, and joy. But we must stay attached to Christ. Men, we stay attached to him by purposely being in his Word with the understanding that this is our daily nourishment that we must feast on.

Just like how a flower in a garden must have good soil, which is natural nourishment, for the flower to bloom and grow into something beautiful, so spiritually, our supernatural soil is in the holy vine, who is Jesus Christ, as I mentioned in the previous sections of the book. Remember, if we abide in him by abiding in his Word, then he will abide in us. That's the holy vine connection to what I'm speaking of.

When we become attached to this supernatural nourishment, we have direct access to a seat at the table. Because Jesus said that everything the Father tells him, Jesus, in return, tells us, and by this we have a seat at the table.

So if we're in the know in the things of the Father, then we will experience and promote in our families and in the world what it means to be created in the image of *God*.

We're living in the era of such tumultuous times with COVID-19, which literally has shut the world down, along with the rioting and shooting of unarmed Black and Brown men, which has provoked protesting over the salvage killings of Black men in the country.

However, with the truth being told, we must understand and know, as Christians, that the prince of this world, the devil, is responsible for all mayhem in America today. He is exercising his satanic power over all those who is blind to his tactics. For he literally has scales over the eyes of all those who have rejected Christ as *Lord* and Savior, which means they become prey for the enemy. But remember this fact right here that we, too, at one time were in the clutches of the devil! Until someone shared the gospel of Jesus Christ with the Holy Spirit, drawing us to him. The only difference was that we accepted him instead of rejecting him. We embraced him as *Lord* and *Savior* of our lives. We did this by acknowledging that Jesus was born of the Virgin Mary, who grew up to be a carpenter's son to Joseph and Mary.

Then in his early thirties, Jesus began his ministry, forthtelling that he would be crucified for the sins of the world. Being crucified on a hill called Golgotha, which in Aramaic means "place of the skull." Jesus was crucified on that hill for the sins of all mankind, yet he rose again on the third day with all power, which defeated death and reconciled all believers who accepted him back to *God*.

Now we have been risen with Christ with all power. The Scripture confirms this account of the story that we believers have been connected with that power. "The Spirit of *God*, who raise Jesus from the dead, lives in you. And just as *God* raised Jesus Christ from the dead, He will give life to your mortal bodies by the same spirit living within you" (Romans 8:11 NLT).

So, men, before we came to know Christ as *Lord* and Savior, as I said, we, too, were blinded by the prince of this world. But thank *God* someone told us about this bloody gospel of Jesus Christ! Share this same good news with those who don't know Christ the same way we were told before we came to Christ.

Since this is a spiritual revelation, we must encounter it in the spiritual realm because the attacks are formulated in the spirit. Well, since the attacks are forge in the spirit, we must confront the enemy, the devil in spirit. When you have White police officers killing unarmed Black men, they are just being blinded by the devil and being used as his operative to carry out these hateful attacks. Now mind you, I'm not saying that all police officers operate in this fashion, for most police officers are good people, and they do serve and protect, plus the fact that they are authorized by *God*.

However, there are a few rogue police officers that are being used by the devil to cause hatred and racial division. We must confront those police officers in the spiritual realm as the Bible tells us to do. "For the weapons of our warfare are not carnal but mighty through

*God* to the pulling down of strong holds; Casting down imaginations, and every high thing that exaleth itself against the knowledge of *God*, and bringing into captivity every thought to the obedience of Christ" (2 Corinthians 10:4–5).

The scripture is very clear on we as Christians must confront the prince of this world—the devil. We confront him in the spiritual realm.

By the way, the devil is already defeated just so you know. It's just that the people who don't know him, they don't know that he's already defeated. But those of us that do know he is a defeated foe, *God* has given us authority over the devil and his imps!

This is why the devil is going after those who are blind to his tactics. The devil also knows his time of causing havoc are coming to an end soon. Why? Because Christ is returning soon. I don't know when he's coming back—in fact, nobody knows when Christ will return to proclaim his church—but we do know his return is imminent, for he is coming back for his church without spot or blemishes. He's coming back to rule and judge the world with all authority and power. We who have confessed and professed that he is the Christ and have accepted him as our *Lord* and Savior, we, too, will be with him to judge the world with all power.

What a glorious day that will be for all who have surrendered their lives over to Christ. So, men, until that day, we must fulfill our purpose on earth, operating in what we were created to do. We were created in the image of *God* to be ambassadors for Christ in a dying and lost world if they don't know Christ. Their only hope is the salvation of Christ being offered to them by the sharing the gospel of Jesus Christ. So we as men of *God* must show our families, our neighbors, our community, our cities, our states, our country, the world what it looks like to represent Christ in his image.

We do that by showing the likeness of Christ in our actions and in our deeds in every fabric of society and in the church and outside the church. So with the question being asked, which is the title of this chapter—what does it mean to be created in the image of *God*? Well, it is to embrace and know that *God* has created us in his image so that people can see Christ in us and through us so that we make

Christ attractive to others so they would want what they see and, in return, get what we have, which is the abundant life offered to us through the gospel. The end result is to spend eternity in heaven with *God* our creator. For we have made Christ attractive to a dying world by operating in the earth in the image and likeness of *God* by making the pages of the Bible come alive through our actions, works, and deeds in the world.

As Apostle Paul said, we are living epistles of the gospel, being read by everyone. But I say, we must give them something to read by making sure we are doers of the Word and not hearers only. Then we can live out what Apostle Paul said on how we are to be living.

They must see the image and the likeness of *God* being displayed in our lives on earth because we are truly living epistles being read by everyone so that we can conclude from this what it means to be created and operating in the image of *God* to his creation. By doing this, we are giving the lost and the downtrodden an opportunity to be reconciled back to *God*.

By representing Christ on earth, when they see us, they don't! They see Christ. Because the image that they are seeing is the likeness and image of *God*.

Listen, men, for some people, the closest they will ever see Christ will be through men of *God* who have surrendered their lives to Christ, as I just mentioned on the previous pages. Yet it bears repeating again in how others must see us when we lead a surrendered life to *God*. Our lives can only be transformed into surrendering to *God*. We do that by our instruction manual, which is the Bible—the divine, holy Word of *God*. When we immerse ourselves in the Word of *God*, our hearts becomes a hiding place for the Word of *God* to set up camp in our hearts.

Remember what King David said about that. Here's what David said: "Thy word have I hid in mine heart, that I might not sin against thee" (Psalm 119:11 KJV).

So, mighty men of *God*, we have to give the world something to read because what they are reading now is not good for them. They are getting most of their information from different news outlets, social media, different sources off the internet. This is why, men, we must have a consecrated life sold out to *God*—so that we can be deployed by *God* strategically throughout our communities, our neighborhoods, our cities, our country, and throughout the world, as I mentioned before. So that we can be read by everyone we come into contact with—that they may see *God* in us and through us on display in our actions and in our deeds.

In order that *God* may be glorified in us and through us, as I stated, the Scripture tells us we were prepared for our roles before the foundation of the world. Here's what the Word of *God* says in our preparedness to do the work of *God* to be read by all men. "For we are *God*'s Masterpiece. He created us anew in Christ Jesus, so we can do good things he planned for us long ago" Ephesians 2:10 NLT).

Wow! Men of *God*, look how the *God* of the universe, the creator of heaven and earth called us. He called us his masterpieces.

What is a masterpiece? According to *Random House Webster's Dictionary Second Edition*, it is "a person's greatest piece of work."

To put it in perspective, when *God* created the world and all that's in it, *God* said, "Let there *be*—" But when it came to creating us! *God* said, "Let *us make mankind* in our image." The *us* represents the Father, the Son, and the Holy Spirit. *God* had a board meeting in heaven with the Triune of *God* and said, "Let us!"

So the Master Creator of the universe has labeled us his creation—his masterpiece—to be deployed in the world to do good works, which he planned before the foundation of the world.

In the next, section we will explore this realization of knowing who we truly are in *God*!

# PART 5

# The Realization of Knowing Who We Are in God

This is the key to living and having a victorious life—knowing who we are in *God*.

The enemy, the prince of the power of the air, his primary function is to distract every child of *God* from seeing their image in *God*. How he does this is simply by attacking the mind with various thoughts and worldly perspectives to distort your image of who you are in *God*.

Listen, this enemy does not care about you and me attending church—he wouldn't even mine at all if you never go to church. But as I was saying, he doesn't care about your church attendance. He doesn't care if you're a choir member or a deacon or an elder or a pastor. You see, just because you attend church doesn't make you a Christian! Now I hear you thinking, *Well, if you're in church, how can the devil deceive me in church?* Remember, the Bible tells us that when Satan was cast out of heaven, he took a third of the angels with him who were in the presence of *God* daily. Now, saints, if he convinced one third of angels to follow him! What chance do we have if we're just church members and not sold out to *God?*

As I stated earlier, just because you attend church doesn't make you and I a Christian. If I can use this analogy—neither does attending college on your scheduled days in the classroom make you a student.

I often use this scenario of going to college but never opening your books to study. Just by going to class doesn't make you a student—same as going to church every Sunday and not reading your Bible does not qualify us to be a Christian. As I just said, just because you're attending classes in college without ever opening your assigned books doesn't make you a college student.

I remember when I attended college, while in class, I would be taking notes from the professors' lectures. This would prepare me for the study and test preparations as well. I recall some students would be of the mindset that they didn't have to study, especially if the professor would say that the upcoming test will be an open-book test.

These students had the mindset that they didn't have to study because of the mere fact that it will be an open-book exam. Why? Because they felt they could just open the book and find the answers.

However, I must point out that taking an open-book test without actually studying is the hardest test possible. Well, for one, it's a time restraint on taking the exam. So if you never opened your book to study, guess what? You will spend majority of your test time trying to find the answers which you don't know where to find—because you don't know where to look, because you never opened up your books. Yet I might add, they fail to study and failed to prepare.

As I mentioned, an open-book test is difficult if you haven't prepared for it. Yet it can be relatively easy if you read the book and prepare beforehand.

The principal thing here is that there must be application to study in order to know that you are not only a student. But you are a good student. This same application applies to studying and reading the Bible to ensure that you are a saved Christian and not just taking up pew space because, when the enemy and the storms of life comes upon you and me, in order for us to weather this storm, our foundation in Christ must be secured. Listen, rest assured the attacks will come and we will need something to draw on. This is why we must be sure that we are saved, as the scripture has laid it out. "Therefore, my brothers and sisters, make every effort to confirm your calling and election. For if you do these things, you will never stumble" (2 Peter 1:10 NIV).

As I was saying, we will need to draw from the well when those attacks come upon us. First, we need to take spiritual inventory of our walk with *God*. Once we have that in order, then we can draw from our source.

The Scripture again gives the meaning of what it is to draw from. The psalmist King David makes it clear in the text. "They word have I hid in mine heart, that I might not sin against thee" (Psalm 119:11 KJV).

Now here's the issue, men, if we haven't opened the Bible and studied for ourselves and the Bible tells us to study and show thyself approved, well, guess what? How would you know what you can hide in your heart and where to find the Word of *God* that is for you to hide?

You see, just going to church sometimes or even on a regular basis is not enough. The devil doesn't mind any of that. As long as you don't know who you are in Christ.

The enemy, the devil, is a roaring lion, seeking permission who he can devour! Well, if you're taking up pew space, you are out there on island all by yourself. In fact, in the wild animal kingdom, the prey that gets caught and devoured are the ones that stray from the pack or family. When if we're just taking up pew space inside the church building and not partaking of the Word of *God*, we put ourselves out there alone on the island of isolation. If so, then the devil will take your lunch and literally beat you down. If you have no knowledge how to defend yourself by the Word of *God*. Once again, as I alluded to earlier in the above passage, we must arm ourselves in the Word of *God*. This Scripture makes it clear on how to do that. "Study to show thyself approved unto *God*, a workman that needeth not to be ashamed, rightly dividing the word of truth" (2 Timothy 2:15 KJV).

This is how we are to validate who we are in *God*. We must study and show thyself approved as the Scripture has suggested. We must know who we are in *God*. We must know the authority we have in *God*. We must know *God's* intentions and the purpose he has for us in the earth realm and over in eternity. We can't know *God* through other folks though. We must know *God* for ourselves. There is a passage in the Bible where an individual thought he could use somebody else's authority in his situation to fight the devil. Saints, we can't be like this individual.

Here's a good example in the Scripture to bring clarity on what I just shared with you. It doesn't matter if we have good church attendance, if you never accepted Christ as *Lord* and Savior or if you became a Christian and never study the Word of *God* by reading the Bible to find out who you are in *God* or if you never know your rights in the kingdom of *God*, you will never be able to access what all you have as a Christian. We can't claim these benefits because your parents walk with *God*.

Here is the good example that I am referring to that will bring clarity of knowing *God* for ourselves. In the book of Acts, there was such a situation where the Father name Sceva a chief priest. One of his sons did work in the church and attended church on a regular basis, yet he didn't know *God* for himself. His son had heard about the Apostle Paul casting out demons in Jesus's name! Men, you can't use this name unless you know him personally. You see, it's one thing to name-drop in the world to get advantage. Yet that's not guaranteeing your success. But to name-drop in the spiritual realm can be dangerous as this son found out. He had encountered an evil spirit, and this was how this son responded. "In the name of Jesus whom Paul preaches, I command you to come out" (Acts 19:13d NIV).

Now, here is where it gets interesting. Here's how the devil responded to this son of Sceva the chief priest:

> And the evil spirit answered and said, Jesus
> I know, and Paul I know, but who are You? Then
> the man who had the evil spirit jumped on them
> and overpowered them, and prevailed against

them, so they fled out of the house naked and wounded. (Acts 19:15–16 NIV/KJV)

Now you see, this is a very clear depiction that just because you have church attendance then folks on the outside think you're a Christian! But you're not!

In this particular text, the priest's sons had no clue what they had in Christ or who they could be in Christ! We're living in an age where the devil is running rampant because he knows his time is coming to an end. Plus the fact that the moment we accept Christ as *Lord* and Savior, we have all authority and power over the devil. Remember, Men of *God*, the devil is a defeated foe.

So, Men of *God*, if we don't know Christ as *Lord* and Savior, as our personal *Lord* and Savior, as I stated earlier, the devil will whip up on us and take our lunch and our lunch money as well as expose our nakedness and have us running for our lives, just like the devil whipped up on the son of Sceva the chief priest. The devil beat him up so bad that he beat his close off him, therefore making him the first recorded streaker in history.

Wow! Think about that, men, how the enemy made all of his sons look utterly ridiculous because one of his sons claimed to know Christ through someone else who actually knew Christ.

Now let's do some self-examination of this text. First, the devil knows everyone who knows Christ personally because he told this particular son, "Jesus I know, Paul I know, but who are you?"

Men, ask yourself—can your name be added to the devil's Rolodex list of saints of someone who knows Christ personally? That also operates in the authority and power and in the anointing of *God*. Well, I'm waiting—can you be added to the list of saints who operate in the authority, anointing, and power of *God*?

This is why this section of this book is so extremely important to every child of *God*, especially to every man of *God* who profess and confess that Jesus is *Lord* over every area of their lives. Do you know who you are in *God*? The Bible already tells us that demons tremble at the name of Jesus.

Now think about this, men! If the demons tremble at the name of Christ and we're supposed to have a relationship with the very person that the demons are afraid of, then why are we acting like the devil has all the power? I'll tell you why—because we don't study our benefit package, the Bible, to find out what we have access to in Christ.

Well, what must we do to rectify that? Exactly! You guessed it! Find out what the Word of *God* says who we are and what we have access to in *God*. Here's what the Word of *God* says about what you and I have access to in having a solid foundation and relationship with Christ. "Everything the Father has is mine. That is what I meant when I said that he [the Holy Spirit] will take things that are mine and reveal [declare, disclose, transmit] it to you" (John 16:15 Amplified Bible, Classic Edition).

This is powerful, men, if you get this in your spirit. What an incredible revelation this is. Did you get it? Let me help you out here. The Scripture says everything that Jesus Christ has, he has now deliberately, purposefully declared, disclosed, and promised to transmit all of that to us.

Men, I'm getting excited right now! Aren't you? Well, you should if you are not. First thing you need to do is to find out what does Christ have that we can have.

Well, let's see. Christ has all authority, all power, all joy, all peace, all abundance, all wealth, all health, all wisdom, all knowledge! Here's the deal, men, we must search the Scripture by doing our due diligence by reading the Bible. Then you can go more in depth in each one of those kingdom benefits I just stated above.

However, just those I just mentioned is enough to get us excited! Those benefits are more than enough to get you and me to surrender our lives all to *God*! Then began to walk in holiness with all that is within us. Once again, the Scripture confirms that, that's our responsibility and part of our Christian walk before *God*.

For the Bible says this, "I beseech you therefor, brethren, by the mercies of *God*, that you present your bodies a living sacrifice, Holy, Acceptable to *God*, which is your reasonable service" (Romans 12:1 NKJV).

The scripture says, men, that it's our reasonable service to walk in holiness before *God*. Plus this magnificent promise that Jesus said that he will transmit all of this power to those who are sold out to him. A transfer of power—think about this analogy that would put this in a better perspective. Every four years, there is a presidential election, and if the incumbent president loses his bid to retain his presidency, one of the most powerful acts that takes place is when the incumbent president greets the newly elected president. There is a transfer of power that takes place for the next four years for the incoming administration.

Well, saints of *God*, the moment we make the *Lord* our Savior by accepting him as Christ, we, too, are involved in a transfer of power, as I have mentioned. But this power from Christ authorized to us will not have a four-year cap on it. Men of *God*, we have this power all the way upon his return! My *God*! Talking about a transfer of power in the spiritual realm—it's called a resurrection power! Plus that Luke 10:19 power that I mentioned before! Wow! We have Power, Men of *God*!

Listen, we must stop trying to figure out *God* and just begin to walk by faith on the Word of *God*. When we do, we will get revelation upon revelation on who we are in *God*, even though we won't have the full revelation of who we are in Christ until we get to heaven.

Yet what we do have access to is the reading of *God's* Word, and what Christ says, we already have base on the Word of *God*. That's enough right there for every man, every woman, every child of *God* to walk in complete authority and power in serving Christ!

For we have been given all authority and power over the kingdom of darkness in every area of society point-blank! This is not negotiable, saints. That's when we become bold in our walk with *God*. You see, that's the devil's biggest fear—that we become aware of who we are in *God*. "For he realized that once we come to the realization of who we are in Christ. The devil and all his imps will have the same reaction to us. The same way they react to Christ presence. Even the demons believe and tremble" (James 2:19c NKJV).

So yes, the devil is fearful of when we will begin to walk in our freedom in Christ by speaking boldly, professing the Word of *God* over our lives, our family, and in the world.

We have all the power over the devil. Remember the scripture I referenced concerning this power earlier. Well, here it is in its context: "Behold I give you the Authority to trample on serpents, and scorpions, and over all the power of the enemy, and nothing shall by any means hurt you" (Luke 10:19 NKJV).

Though we have all power given to us by Jesus Christ, yet he told the disciples this statement right here: "However do not rejoice that the spirits submit to you, but rejoice that your names are written in heaven" (Luke 10:20 NIV).

Now this same statement that Jesus told his disciples also applies to every man, every woman, and, once again, every child of *God*.

If I can unpack the Scripture above for a moment, Christ is saying here that though he has given us all power over the devil and his imps, though they submit to us, Christ is saying, "That's not what I want you to be happy about. What I want you to be happy about is that your names are written in the lamb's book of life."

In other words, get happy knowing you will spend eternity with the Father in heaven. Jesus wants us to remain humble in our walk with him. Despite the fact that we have overcome the world because Christ has overcome the world.

This is what Jesus was trying to share with his disciples—that the true miracle is that we believed in the name of Jesus Christ and we are accepted in the beloveds of him, our Savior because of his death, burial, and resurrection, which is the gospel of Jesus Christ. Now listen, men, that is truly something to rejoice about. It truly is! Jesus is saying, "Rejoice in this fact that you believed on me and confessed your sins before my Father. And because of this, we have been forgiven and reconciled back to *God*. Because of this fact, Men of *God*, we will now spend eternity with Christ reigning forever!" Now that is truly something to rejoice about! That once, we were dead in our trespasses and sins, and because we accepted the gospel, we have been reunited back to the father. We rejoice because of this! This is the good news, saints! This is what we should be rejoicing about.

Now because we are reconciled back to the Father, we now have power and authority over the kingdom of darkness, which is the devil's and his imps. Because of this authorized power, we as believers live the blessed life, for the power we received from Jesus Christ is just the by-product that is only available to the believer, for we have accepted Christ as *Lord* and Savior over our lives!

In fact, I want to pause for a moment in my writing. I want to offer the plan of salvation to anyone who is reading this book, who doesn't know Jesus Christ as *Lord* and Savior. Repeat this after me:

> Dear *Lord*, I believe that you died on Calvary for all my sins. I believe that you died and rose on the third day. Please forgive me for my sins. Come into my heart and save me *Lord*. From this day forward, I will follow you and obey you. Thank you, Jesus.

Now at this point, get into a church that teaches the gospel of Christ. You can also ask the *Lord* to direct you to a church where your faith can be nurtured and grown! You are now saved! You may feel nothing. But trust me, you are saved!

Guess what? Because the decision that you just made and that those of us who already made this decision, our names are now written in lamb's book of life! Which is truly the only reason that we should be rejoicing, as I have mentioned in the above paragraphs.

Now back to elaborating on why Jesus said why we should be rejoicing. Jesus wanted his disciples to understand to temper their excitement in regard to the evil spirits bowing down to them, even though that is also good news. He wanted his disciples and you and me to keep our priorities in order, where our rejoicing should be applied to.

Jesus never wanted us to lose our humility in our walk with *God*. You see, in the world, they look at humility as being weak. In the spiritual realm, humility in serving Christ is simply having authority under control. In other words, being a Christian isn't a sign of weakness. On the contrary, it is a sign of strength.

Men, remember this was Jesus's attitude when he was facing Pontius Pilate before his crucifixion, even though Jesus had the power and authority to stop his crucifixion. Instead, he humbled himself unto death for our sake on the cross.

That is why we as Men of *God* must follow the example of Christ, which is to be humbled in our God Given Authority and always remember what our rejoicing should be about—that our names are written in heaven in the lamb's book of life.

We will be forever spending eternity with the Father who art in heaven where we will be praising and worshiping *God* for eternity!

Now, Men of *God*, with this understanding, we get more clarity and become more aware of the realization of knowing who we are in Christ. We are the exact image of Christ from inception, which is that we were created in the image of *God* from the very beginning.

With that being the case, we were created to rule and multiply on earth and have dominion over everything in the earth and in the sea. But because of the fall of the first Adam, sin entered in the world. The second Adam, Jesus Christ, had to come and reconcile mankind back to *God* so that we could be reestablished to *God*'s original covenant, which he made with the first Adam.

Now that we have been reunited with Christ, we have that same command to have dominion on the earth.

But we have a new addendum to the original covenant he made with Adam. This new addendum includes that we become spiritual fishermen in sharing the gospel of Christ to the lost and downtrodden of humanity, sharing with the lost that Christ is the answer, also sharing with them why Christ is the answer for the world today and still operate in the original covenant that *God* gave Adam, which is still to have dominion and authority in this world and for you and me to never lose sight of this, as well as what our true rejoicing should be about.

Though we are to carry out the original covenant that *God* gave Adam in the garden, which is to have dominion in the world, to increase upon increase, to replenish and subdue in the earth. Yet our rejoicing and joy should be that our names are written in the lamb's book of life. Remember, this is what Jesus told the disciples on what their true joy should be about. When they came back, proudly sharing how even the demons submits to their *God*-given authority, this is what Jesus reminded them of and for us too. This reminder is for us as well. "But don't rejoice because of evil spirits obey you; Rejoice because your names are registered in heaven" (Luke 10:20 NLT).

Now, men of *God*, Jesus wasn't saying, "Don't be excited about the victories you have because of me." We are not trying to get victories. We already have the victory because of Calvary. Men of *God*, Calvary changes everything!

But Jesus knew we must never forget or lose sight of what we were before we came to Christ. But look at where we are now, even though we're still a work in progress.

The fact is we are now in Christ and our names are written in the lamb's book of life, which is the most important decision we ever made, which is to follow Christ and accept him as *Lord* and Savior of our lives.

Jesus knew that our excitement and joy should solely rest upon our salvation, which will remind each of us what we have now so that when we share this gospel with the lost, our compassion level for the lost will be on high alert.

That we show compassion on them! Just like when someone showed compassion on us when we were introduced to Christ. That is when the realization of knowing who we are in *God* because of what we have in *God* comes in. What we have in *God* is full authority by having access to the keys of the kingdom, which is to bind and lose the supernatural into the natural, which is earth. I want to make this clear, Men of *God*. There is binding and loosing in heaven. This is a supernatural act carried out in an earthly function.

We have the peace of *God* that will enable each of us to live a life of fruitfulness in the Spirit. This peace of *God* that we have access to transcends through every challenge that we face, every obstacle and the fact we do not process bad news like the world. Why? We have access to inexplicable joy that the world did not give us because this joy comes from the *Lord*.

Despite what we have in Christ, we do not live a life free from trouble or conflicts and challenges. Yet we have this immutable promise from *God* concerning this life on earth—that no matter the affliction we face in the world, here is what Scripture says about that:

"Many are the afflictions of the righteous. But the *Lord* delivers him out of them all" (Psalm 34:19 NKJV).

Listen, last time, I looked up the definition of *all*, it is always more than some! When *God* says all, he means just that. Listen, there are times in our lives that *God* proves himself to us, not because he needs to but because he chooses to do just that because he is *God* and he is *God* all by himself.

To prove this point, there are times that *God* will choose not to deliver us out of our trials and tribulations. But he will choose to deliver us in the situation. In fact, you are right—the Scripture bears witness of this fact too. "When you pass through the waters, I will be with you; and when you pass through the rivers. They will not sweep over you. When you walk through the fire you will not be burned; the flames will not set you ablaze" (Isaiah 43:2 NIV/KJV).

Men, lets unpack this scripture. Look at all the perils that we face. Yet notice that we are not staying put. But we are going through some stuff. We are going through the waters. That, in the natural, looks like it will overtake us. But *God* says, "Keep walking. Do not get distracted by the noise. Keep walking, saints! Now the fire is coming. The enemy is turning up the heat like he did on Shadrach, Meshach, and Abednego."

Let the enemy turn the heat up! It is not going to burn us. But it will burn the enemy. Jesus said, "Keep walking for the fire will not set us ablaze."

In other words, what got on you will not stay on you. You will not look like what you went through. We will not even smell like smoke. On the fourth of July, I was grilling barbecue, and the smell of the charcoal and the barbecue got in my clothes. I smelled like what I was doing. But Jesus promised us though the fire is blazing, keep walking!"

*God* is setting us up to remind each of us. We already have the victory! We are not trying to get the victory. For when we come out of the fire, then *God* will see his reflection in us!

Then we will come into the realization of knowing who we are in *God*. And what we have in *God*. Now is the time to start executing *God's* plan to operate in his image!

# PART 6

# Executing God's Plan While Operating in the Image of God

Well, men, we now have come to the conclusion, which is executing *God's* plan of operating in his image in the earth.

Let us do a quick recap of what I shared thus far.

First, we explored together getting to know *God* through the Scripture. This is the foundation in our walk and growth in *God*.

Second, the process of discovering the essence of *God* through the *God*-inspired scriptures written by men of *God*.

Third, from there, we traveled through the Scripture, searching *God's* original plans and purpose for each man who confess and profess our allegiance to *God*.

Fourth, we discovered the impact on each of us on what it means to be created in the image of *God*.

Fifth, we journeyed down the road concerning the aspect on the realization of believing who you are in *God*.

And now, let us get into the conclusion of the matter—the biblical perspective concerning the application in operating in the image of *God*. When we fully embrace what it means to be created in his image, we can then begin operating and executing *God*'s plans for our lives as men of *God*.

What is *God*'s plan? Well, it is, to be the answer and solution in a fallen world because of Satan, who is the prince of the air. Men, we become the answer and solution by being the salt and light in this dark world. We become the answer and the solution by being doers of the Word instead of hearers only. The Bible makes that clear on how we should operate in this world. I mentioned that the devil is the prince of the air. The reason why the enemy is called that, the Scripture indicates this. "But for twenty-one days the spirit prince of the Kingdom of Persia blocked my way. Then Michael, one of the Archangels, came to help me, and I left him there with the prince of the Kingdom of Persia" (Daniel 10:13 NLT).

What the text is saying is that the original messenger of *God* got caught up in the air with the prince of Persia, the devil. The scripture indicates that Michael, one the archangels, had to come free up the original messenger of *God*.

The devil has some authority. But he doesn't have the ultimate authority. Though his authority is limited, yet he has many people blinded to the things and ways of *God*.

That's where we become the answer and solution, men of *God*. We do this by being *God*'s representative on the earth, by operating in the image that *God* created us.

*God* has ordained and equipped each child of *God* with authority and absolute power to rebuke all devils and demons. We have been endorsed by *God* to do just that, as it is outlined in the scriptures. *God* has given great detail of this power we have over the devil and his imps in the world. "Behold, I given you authority to tread on serpents and scorpions, and upon all the power of the enemy, and nothing will injure you" (Luke 10:19 NASB).

Men, do you really grasp the enormity and truth of *God*'s Word in this scripture? Do you really? For *God* has given us all authority and all power over the devil and all his imps.

Then *God* gave us a bonus in the Scripture when he said that by no means will we be harmed. Men of *God*, when we operate in this capacity, we are not fighting for the victory. We are already operating from a place of victory, for we are operating in the truth of the scripture. For the devil is defeated, and *God* is exalted. Though he may operate as the prince of the air. Though he is defeated, yet the devil has blinded those who do not know *God*. Consequently, they do not know that the devil is a defeated foe.

This is why it is so important for the believers to know who you are in Christ. We can't be pew sitters only. We must apply the Word of *God* to our lives. If not, then we are susceptible to the tricks of the devil. For he will blind the people who profess and confess to know *God*. But their actions speak otherwise. The enemy, the devil, will use distractions, induce fear, and have people come against you being used by him, whether they be folks in your family or folks in your church who operate from a religious point of view, instead of operating from having a proven relationship with *God*.

We must be prepared to face all opposition that the world may throw our way. We do this by communicating with *God* daily and by prayer every morning.

This is where our daily strength comes from. When we purposely and deliberately go after *God* by communing through prayer. The Scripture tell us the reason why we should go before *God* daily in prayer. "And He spake a parable unto them to this end, that men ought always to pray, and not to faint" (Luke 18:1 KJV).

Just the simplicity of this text should be taken as face value. We must pray first, which is a command wrapped in a suggestion, yet strongly implied.

Because Jesus gave each of us free will, the decision to have a daily prayer life solely depends on the individual. Now here is the thing, men. If Jesus prayed and he is the model for us how and when we should pray, well, I don't know about you, but I will definitely follow his lead and pray.

Second, there is an end result concerning our prayers. For they will be answered on his time, not our time. In the book of Habakkuk, there is a scripture confirming that our prayers, our visions, our request will not go unanswered. "For the vision is yet for appointed time; But at the end it will speak, and it will not lie, though it tarries, wait for it; Because it will surely come, it will not tarry" (Habakkuk 2:3 NKJV).

*God* is saying that though it may tarry, he also promised that the answer is on the way. If we do not pray, we will be weak at the knees and we will not be able to handle the blows of the enemy. We will faint in the struggle. Yet the opposite will take place when we do pray—we will walk in peace with the guidance of the Holy Spirit. The Holy Spirit allows us to have a seat at the table. Remember, in the Bible, it gives the distinct role of the Holy Spirit. Jesus said that the Holy Spirit doesn't speak on his own accord. He only speaks what he hears. Then the Holy Spirit comes to inform those of us who choose to be led by the Holy Spirit. The Scripture tells us that he will guide us in all truth.

Now because the Holy Spirit sits at the table, so do we when we faithfully submit to the will of *God*. We do this by communing daily with *God* through prayer and reading the Word daily. For this to become a part of our daily life. We must comply with our obedience to be doing just that, which is actively and faithfully reading our Bibles and praying. Then we start the day filled with Holy Ghost's power. So whenever we leave our physical residence, we will be suited and booted in the things of *God*.

By putting on our spiritual armor to combat against the schemes of the devil, when we as men of *God* actively go after *God* in prayer and read the Word of *God*, we can then begin to implement the things of *God* daily in our lives. When this takes place, we begin to operate in the image that we were created from, which is *God*.

You know, it's just like this analogy of being born into our natural family. For example, my parents who are both resting in the bosom of *God*, their last name was Thomas, which means I was born a Thomas. I have or should have certain DNA traits that can be only be associated with my father and mother. So as I grew from infant to childhood into my adult years, there should be some physical resemblance that I belong to them, as well as my voice, my behavior, or the way I do things. It all should resemble the way my dad has done things and the way my mom has done things. Our thinking should be in the same value of life. Sometimes, we can have the same attributes from both parents. So even as we grow in maturity, we should exhibit some of our parents' traits because of our DNA.

There were moments in my life where I did not exhibit my dad or mom's DNA. Why? Because the lifestyle that I was living didn't reveal any of the Thomas attributes because of my previous lifestyle of drugs taken and sold. Yet despite all that I was doing, though the things I was doing were not pleasing to them, my parents still love me because of their unfailing love toward me. And listen, because of this unfailing love being shown toward me by my parents, I began to show through my actions that I belong to the Thomas family.

So I began to show attributes of being a Thomas by doing right things in my life. The main right thing that I have done was to stop doing drugs. I went back to my life as a Christian. By the way, I accepted Christ as my *Lord* and Savior at the age of thirteen. I was blessed—both my parents saw me become a servant of the most high *God*.

I became an ordained and licensed elder in the Church of *God* in Christ. Now mind you, the moment I accepted Christ, I was engrafted in the family of *God* at thirteen. So my Christian walk with *God* in the beginning started off with fire. Then I fell off the horse and my growth in Christ became stagnated. I stopped growing, as we all have in our lives for every reason to stop growing. For whatever reason we stop growing in the things of *God* is because life's distractions have infiltrated our lives. These life distractions just do not happen by themselves. Oftentimes, these are choices by us. We stop reading our Bibles. We stop communicating with *God* in prayer, which will allow the enemy access to our mental real estate, the spirit of our minds. Just so you know, that part of us, the ear, is the spiritual high-rent district that belongs to *God*.

When the enemy belongs under our feet and not in our ears, yet even in our falling off from *God*, he still loves us perfectly because of his perfect, steady love. I began to get back in prayer, praying more. I started to act like I belong to *God* and that he is my Father. I began to show attributes in life that I belong to *God*. We will know we have these attributes by our actions and deeds in the *Lord*. The Bible speaks on this. It is called fruit bearing. What kind of fruits are we bearing?

The Scripture tells us we will be known by the fruits we produce. So how we live will manifest what our life is showing to others. "So I say, live by the spirit" (Galatians 5:16b Life Application Bible).

Men of *God*, when we walk in the spirit, we most definitely will be living by the spirit. Now what kind of spirit will you be representing is the question. The fruit of the spirit will be evident in every man who humbles himself before the *Lord*.

When we do this as Men of *God*, here is the result of our submission to the Father. "But the fruit of the spirit is love, Joy, Peace, Patience, Kindness, Goodness, Faithfulness, gentleness and self-control" (Galatians 5:22–23d).

There is power and anointing when we as men operate in these fruits of the Spirit of *God*. We will begin to operate in this way daily. Then the world will know we belong to *God*.

The enemy will have no power over any man who willingly choose to live a surrendered life unto *God*. Let me share this quote again from Robert Murray M'Cheyne, who said, "A Holy Minister is an Awful weapon in the Hand of *God*."

This powerful statement, men, can be applied to our lives as well. For you and I to operate in this kind of anointing, nothing less than a surrendered life to Christ our *Lord* will do.

Only a surrendered life will make us pliable in the master's hand and in that hand as Robert Murray M'Cheyne so eloquently stated above. When he said a holy minister is an awful weapon in the hand of *God*, we, too, can become an awful weapon in the hand of *God*.

You know, oftentimes in the military, special forces like the marines or the Navy seals are deployed on certain missions because of their special skill sets for a particular mission. Well, *God* will deploy any man whose life is surrendered unto him, for we can now be used by *God* to tear down the kingdom of darkness—remember I mentioned before that we were created by *God* to do good works before the foundation of the world.

For *God* called us his masterpieces, so we are ordained to do great things in *God*. I also mentioned in the previous chapter that we are *God*'s answer to the devil who was kicked out of heaven, along with one third of the heavenly hosts.

What I am saying, men, is that *God* has given each man who has surrendered to his will all we need to be used by *God* to tear down the kingdom of darkness.

*God* has given us all power, for he is the source of this power. However, the power will only flow through unobstructed spiritual conduit. In other word, this power will only flow if we stay connected to the power source, which is *God*. We are the conduit by which that power flows. The only thing that will block that power from flowing is you and me. We block this flow when we stop feeding our spirit man daily in the Word of *God*, by not praying to *God* daily, which is our communication with *God*. Also, when we fail to commune with the Holy Spirit. Now, men, ask yourself this question—why do we not commune with the Holy Spirit daily when Jesus left us the Holy Spirit to guide us in all truth

We live in a depraved and sinful, fallen world where the prince of this world has blinded them who do not know him or who do not believe in *God* or trust the church. We are the salt of the earth! Our mandate is to make people who do not know *God* to become thirsty for *God* whom we know and faithfully serve.

Men of *God*, we can only do this by the way Apostle Paul boldly proclaimed he did—a bond servant of Jesus Christ. In other words, Paul was sold out for the cause of Christ! We must also be sold out for the cause of Christ, which means we become under attacked by the enemy. For the attacks will come. The enemy, Satan, always opposes what *God* will accomplish through you and me as yielded vessels.

The moment doors begin to open up to do ministry before *God*, the enemy will always try to oppose it. The Scripture once again reveals this to us. "Because a great door for effective work has opened to me, and there are many who oppose me" (1 Corinthians 16:9 NIV).

Listen, though they maybe opposition, the Bible clearly states this fact. When *God* opens the door, he will enable his yielded vessels to go through despite the opposition. For the effective door has been opened. We will be victorious because of Christ. Remember this text that clearly outlines our victories. "Now thanks be to *God* who always leads us in triumph in Christ" (2 Corinthians 2:14a NKJV).

I want to point out one word in the text above that crushes all opposition—"*Always*."

Men! *God* is saying that despite the opposition, *God* will always cause us to triumph because of him. One of my favorite anointed gospel songs is "Victory Belongs to Jesus" by Todd Dulaney.

I love this song! So yes, men of *God*! That is the good news—that victory belongs to Jesus!

Guess what, men of *God*? Because we belong to Jesus, the victory belongs to you and me as well. Yes, the victory will always belong to us when we continue to operate in the tenets of the Scripture.

This is what it means to execute *God's* plans on the earth. We will begin to operate in the image of *God*. For greater is *he* that is inside of us than he that is in the world. The all-sovereign *God*, the creator of the universe, who spoke the world into existence by his Word. We have this very nature of *God* in us, men!

The awesomeness of *God* is unfathomable to the human mind! Yet it is to be in awe of.

Let me share with you an event that brought me into that realization—that *God* is *God* and he is *God* all by himself and that *God* alone is to be recognized as the only one to be in awe of.

Several years ago when I was married, my wife and I, at that time, drove down to Arizona to visit the Grand Canyon. Upon our arrival, we settled in for the evening before heading out to view the Grand Canyon in the morning. We checked into on the West Rim Hotel of the Grand Canyon, which by the way has three rims.

I can recall the excitement and the anticipation of seeing the Grand Canyon in all its awesomeness. Some of the stories that you hear about the Grand Canyon is that people have been overdrawn to its awesomeness and committed suicide. Of course, we know that was a trick of the enemy, the devil.

So as I proceeded to go down the trail of the west rim of the Canyon, I remember walking down the trail of the Grand Canyon and I began to feel overwhelmed at the enormity and the vastness of the Grand Canyon. I'm talking to the point—my knees were beginning to get weak from my initial experience walking down the trail.

Then I remember that as I was beginning to walk back up the trail to regain my composure, the Holy Spirit spoke to me and said, "Don't be in awe of the Grand Canyon but be in awe of me who created the Grand Canyon."

When I got back to the top, I began to worship the *Lord* in all its beauty and his majesty. As I was immersed in worshipping the living *God*, I now had a different outlook over the Grand Canyon. When I focused on the awesomeness of *God*, realizing that his baby finger could fill up all the rims of the Grand Canyon, reminding myself that *God* alone is worthy of all the praises and the glory that he alone is due.

For *God* alone is worthy of all the glory. I could now appreciate the beauty and magnificent of *God*'s beauty in the Grand Canyon. From that day on, I will always be reminded of the majestic awesomeness of *God*. I think of this Scripture right here in the book of Psalm that reveals the awesomeness of *God*.

> O *Lord* my *God*, You are very great; You are clothe with honor and majesty. Who cover Yourself with light as with a garment; Who stretches out the heavens like a curtain. He lays the beams of his upper chambers in the waters. Who makes the clouds his chariot, Who walks on the wings of the wind, Who makes his angels spirits, His Ministers flames of fire. You who laid the foundations of the earth, So that it should not be moved forever. (Psalm 104:1–5 NKJV)

When I read this text, it is a constant reminder of the awesomeness of *God*. What a mighty *God* we serve! The Grand Canyon is no match for the majesty and the awesomeness of *God*.

So, men, in conclusion, we are called to execute the plans of *God* on the earth by operating in the image of *God*.

Listen, no matter the opposition that Apostle Paul talked about when the door of effectiveness is open to us or even being overwhelmed like I felt that morning, and I'm sure many of you have felt overwhelmed, especially in this pandemic season of COVID-19, one can easily be overwhelmed if *God* is not your rock during these tumultuous times, along with all the racial upheaval and all the injustices in the world. Yes, if one is not careful and watch the news and social media as your main diet of information, instead focusing and trusting *God*, you will be overwhelmed.

Yet the moment I began to acknowledge *God* and began to worship *God* in the beauty of his holiness and being reminded of who *God* is as opposed to who we are. For *God* is our creator as the scripture reveals to us, "Know that the *Lord* is *God* it is he who made us, and we are his" (Psalm 100:3 NIV).

Men of *God*, as we began to walk in our defined roles and purpose in *God*, we will now begin to operate what it is to be a man of *God*, being ordained by *God* to be his answer in this world. Men, *God* is still speaking the clarion call, as he has called out on Adam, "Where are you?" We know Adam was hiding. Men, we don't need to be hiding anymore. Come out from the among them in the world. We must be bold for the *Lord*. We must run to the *Lord*, not run from the *Lord*. Our response when we hear the call should be, "Here, *Lord*, I am here. Use me, *Lord*."

Then we can have our *Ta-Da* moment. Yes, you know the moment like in the old vaudeville acts when the major act is getting ready to come to the stage. While the curtains are closed, you hear all this noise behind the curtain. It is the stage crew getting things in order to present the major act to the stage.

When the major act comes on, when the curtains are pulled back, the presenter finally shouts out, "*Ta-da!*"

Well, men of *God*, once we surrender our lives to *God*, he has us in the backstage of life, preparing us and shaping us, like he did when he told Jeremiah to go down to the potter's house and look inside. As Jeremiah looked inside, the *Lord* came up to him and said, "O house of Israel, can I not do with you as the potter? Says the *Lord*. Look, as the clay is in the potter's hand, so are you in my Hand" (Jeremiah 18:6 NKJV).

So, men of *God*, when we submit to the will of *God*, he will mold us and shape us, and when we are shaped into his will, then *God* will pull back the curtains of life and present us to the world by saying, "*Ta-da*." Yes, we will be *t*errifically *a*nointed and *d*ivinely *a*ppointed—TA-DA!

I pray this book will guide you and me along the way—that the world may know that we belong to *God*, that we are Men of *God* being deployed on the earth to tear down the kingdom of darkness by operating in the kingdom of *God*, who will always cause you and me to triumph. To *God* be the glory! Amen!

# ACKNOWLEDGMENTS

Special thanks to Elder Joe Brown (RIP), who exemplified what it is to be a man of integrity and strength and to love and take care of your family—A True Man of God.

I want to thank my former pastor, Bishop Edward G. Mehaclan (RIP), who taught me and trained me in the things of God and to be sensitive to the Holy Spirit and who ordained me as the chairman of the deacon board, then an ordained minister, and then ordained into the eldership, all in the church of God in Christ.

And truly a special thanks to one of the greatest Gospel preachers (if not the best), my pastor, Apostle Ronald C. Hill, and the most gracious First Lady (my co-pastor), Osie L. Hill, in all of Christendom. Both of these anointed leaders have greatly impacted my life to walk in holiness and sharing the Gospel with the lost and downtrodden and to whomsoever will accept Christ as Lord and Savior.

I don't know any other pastor who wins souls for the kingdom of God than my pastor, Apostle Ron C. Hill, who implores every member to read our Bibles and fast and pray and fast and pray and read our Bibles. I love you both, and may God continue to bless you both over to abundance in every area of your lives.

# REFERENCES

1843–1921. *New Scofield Study Bible-KJV Editor.*

2015. *Amplified Bible.* Lockman Foundation.

*Amplified Bible, Classic Edition (AMPC).* Lockman Foundation.

*Holy Bible—English Standard Version (ESV).* Bible Gateway.

*Holy Bible—New King James Version (NKJV).* Bible Gateway Online Version.

*New American Standard Bible (NASB).* Lockman Foundation.

*New Living Testament (NLT).* Tyndale online version.

Thompson, Frank Charles, DD, PhD. *Thomas Chain-References Bible: New International Version (NIV).*

Wiersbe, Warren Wendall. An American Christian clergyman and Bible teacher.

# ABOUT THE AUTHOR

He was born and raised in California and grew up in the great city of Compton. His parents set the greatest example in strength and fortitude for him and his siblings—his sister, Denise Lynn Powell, and his brother, Darrell Wayne Thomas—in shaping them to be Men and Women of God as they are today! His mother, Evangelist Mary L. Thomas, imputed in him sensitivity and compassion by the love she poured out in their hearts, and his dad, Marion Jhiniah Thomas Sr., imputed in him a sense of responsibility and family, which both represent love.

The greatest example of that love is when his dad married his mom, he took in her brothers and sister and raised them along with him and his siblings as a family—his uncles, Ezra Carbins, Dr. Eddie Carbins (RIP), Charles Carbins (RIP), Willie Carbins (RIP), Marion Calhoun, and his aunt, Ida (RIP), director of nursing, were all raised under the tutelage and guidance from his dad!

Both of his parents are now resting in the presence of God, and this author knows fully well he will see them again when the Lord returns for his church! The bedrock of his foundation as a person rests on those two principles exhibited by his mom and dad, so he patterned his life in showing compassion and sensitivity from his Mom and strength from his Dad!

He has two children whom he is very proud of—his son, Marion J. Thomas III, who is forty, and his daughter, Samantha Grace Thomas, who is eighteen.

All of his family played an important role in his development to be the Man of God he is today! He was introduced to Jesus Christ at an early age and accepted him as the Lord and Savior of his life, and when you think about it, Christ himself is full of compassion, sensitivity, and strength and family, which was on display in his household all his life!

He loves God, and he loves God's people. The anointing is on his life, and he is destined to reign in Christ and with Christ to fulfill the calling that God has on his life by operating in the kingdom principles that God has ordained for him as the man of God, representing him on the earth by sharing the gospel to the lost and to fulfill his purpose ordained on his life by the living God.

CPSIA information can be obtained
at www.ICGtesting.com
Printed in the USA
BVHW032028100323
660178BV00002B/464